D0872394

Gender Politics and the Olympic Industry

DOI: 10.1057/9781137291158

Also by Helen Jefferson Lenskyj

PALGRAVE HANDBOOK OF OLYMPIC STUDIES (*co-edited with Stephen Wagg*)

OLYMPIC INDUSTRY RESISTANCE: Challenging Olympic Power and Propaganda

OUT ON THE FIELD: Gender, Sport and Sexualities

THE BEST OLYMPICS EVER? Social Impacts of Sydney 2000

INSIDE THE OLYMPIC INDUSTRY: Power, Politics and Activism

OUT OF BOUNDS: Women, Sport and Sexuality

DOI: 10.1057/9781137291158

palgrave▸**pivot**

Gender Politics and the Olympic Industry

Helen Jefferson Lenskyj
University of Toronto, Canada

DOI: 10.1057/9781137291158

First published 2013 by
PALGRAVE MACMILLAN

Palgrave Macmillan in the UK is an imprint of Macmillan Publishers Limited, registered in England, company number 785998, of Houndmills, Basingstoke, Hampshire RG21 6XS.

Palgrave Macmillan in the US is a division of St Martin's Press LLC, 175 Fifth Avenue, New York, NY 10010.

Palgrave Macmillan is the global academic imprint of the above companies and has companies and representatives throughout the world.

Palgrave® and Macmillan® are registered trademarks in the United States, the United Kingdom, Europe and other countries.

ISBN: 978-1-137-29116-5 EPUB
ISBN: 978-1-137-29115-8 PDF
ISBN: 978-1-137-29114-1 Hardback

A catalogue record for this book is available from the British Library.

A catalog record for this book is available from the Library of Congress.

www.palgrave.com/pivot

DOI: 10.1057/9781137291158

Contents

Acknowledgements   vi

1   Introduction   1

2   Beyond Binaries: An Intersectional
    Analysis   11

3   The Limits of Liberalism: Sex, Gender
    and Sexualities   39

4   Challenges to the Olympic Industry   52

5   In the Pool, on the Ice: Contested Terrain   87

6   Sex and the Games   108

7   Conclusion   131

Bibliography   137

Index   153

Acknowledgements

Some parts of this book have been in the making since the 1980s, and so there are many people to thank. Over the years, my thinking on issues of gender politics and the Olympics has greatly benefited from discussions and debates with family, friends and colleagues in Canada, the US, the UK and Australia. In the course of my research since 1999, I've interviewed Olympic athletes, investigative journalists and community activists, and I'm grateful to them for their time and, above all, for their commitment to social justice. Don McLeod of the Canadian Lesbian and Gay Archives kindly provided me with the unpublished draft of his annotated bibliography of Canadian gay and lesbian periodicals. Thanks are due to Palgrave Macmillan staff and editor Philippa Grand, who supported the project from the outset, and to the anonymous reader for helpful comments. I am grateful to Talia Linz for her work on compiling the bibliography, and to my partner, Liz Green, for valuable feedback and expert proofreading. As always, I thank my partner Liz and my children for their love and support.

DOI: 10.1057/9781137291158

1
Introduction

Abstract: *This chapter discusses the author's background and the experiences that inform the theoretical and methodological approach used in the book, that is, an intersectional analysis of gender politics and the Olympic industry. A rationale for the structure of the book and an overview of each chapter are provided, as well as an explanation of the scope and limits of the research.*

Lenskyj, Helen Jefferson. *Gender Politics and the Olympic Industry*. Basingstoke: Palgrave Macmillan, 2013. DOI: 10.1057/9781137291158.

In 1985, when I was writing *Out of Bounds: Women, Sport and Sexuality*, an analysis of the history of women and sport in Canada, the US and the UK from the 1890s to the 1980s, I was guided by radical feminist Adrienne Rich's concept of compulsory heterosexuality, in combination with neo-Marxist insights concerning "common sense" and hegemony.[1] In short, as I would have summarized it at the time, the history of western women and sport is a history of male control over middle-class female sexuality, with the growth of women's sport viewed by the ruling gender-class as a threat to patriarchal hegemony.

Following its publication, one favourable review noted that the book served as a "Rosetta Stone" that helped to decode a century of constraints on women in sport.[2] I am now undertaking a similar decoding of Olympic history by broadening my original focus on what contemporary theorists term "heteronormativity."[3] The use of gender or sexuality as sole categories of analysis risks perpetuating "the whiteness of sport studies and queer scholarship," as Mary McDonald demonstrated in a 2006 article that critiqued, among other examples, Pat Griffin's 1998 book *Strong Women, Deep Closets* and my 2003 book *Out on the Field: Gender, Sport and Sexualities.*[4] As McDonald rightly noted, although the importance of an intersectional focus, looking at race, sexuality, class and nation, was mentioned, that analysis was not fully developed in either book.[5]

Much has changed in critical sport scholarship since the 1980s, and the theoretical insights of the past three decades need to be taken into account. These developments have been influenced by significant work in critical race studies, globalization studies, transnational feminist theory, cultural studies, queer theory and various interdisciplinary fields. Since the categories of sex, gender and sexuality are further complicated by race/ethnicity and social class, they need to be considered in more nuanced ways if they are to have explanatory value in relation to the Olympic industry.

My first direct encounter with the Olympic industry occurred in 1990 when I was contracted to write a research report on the status of women in the Summer Olympics for the City of Toronto Olympic Task Force. In the late 1980s, Toronto was organizing its bid for the 1996 Olympics, the first of two unsuccessful attempts to date. Around the same time, I heard about the Bread Not Circuses (BNC) coalition, a group of community organizations that was opposing the Toronto bid. Its position was grounded in a socialist analysis of the negative impacts of the Olympic Games and other sport mega-events on vulnerable populations

DOI: 10.1057/9781137291158

in the host city and region, as well as the drain on public money, the environmental impacts and the threat to human rights.[6] In 1998, when Toronto was bidding for the 2008 Olympics, I joined BNC, just months before the International Olympic Committee (IOC) bribery scandals were exposed, and the rest, as they say, is history.

A 1992 conference paper on community involvement in Toronto's 1996 Olympic bid process marked the beginning of my research on a set of social institutions that I term "the Olympic industry." As I have explained in earlier work, I use the term "industry" to draw attention to the fact that sporting competition is the mere tip of the gigantic Olympic industry iceberg. Profit-making is the name of the game, and the International Olympic Committee, multinational sponsors, broadcast rights holders, real estate developers and the high end of the hospitality and tourism industries take home the gold. These aspects of the Olympic industry are largely concealed from view, thanks to a generously funded public relations machine supported by largely uncritical mainstream media.

In my critical Olympic research since 1992, I have examined issues of gender and sexuality, and in my research on gender and sport, I include Olympic-related topics. This book brings all these themes together. The scope is broader than my work on sport and gender, in that I pay particular attention to intersectionality, that is, interlocking systems of oppression based on gender, sexuality, social class, race and ethnicity, as played out in Olympic governance, international and national sports organizations, the mass media and the sport community. In existing research on historical and contemporary issues in women's sport, as well as in western sport feminists' political organizing, there is a longstanding pattern of reliance on a liberal analysis of women and the Olympics and an emphasis on reform, trends that I have critiqued extensively in the past. In the following chapters, I use insights from transnational feminism, radical feminism, critical race theory and cultural studies to continue that critique and to expose aspects of discrimination and oppression that have often been neglected in Olympic studies, sport sociology and sport history research. In doing so, I uncover the connections among these systems and the opportunities for resistance.

Over a span of more than 30 years, my work has reflected a combination of qualitative research methods, including participant observation in Canadian and Australian anti-Olympic groups, and interviews with recreational and elite athletes, activists, community leaders, environmentalists, housing advocates and investigative journalists. In addition,

DOI: 10.1057/9781137291158

I have conducted content analysis of print and visual media sources, archival research and online investigation of resistance movements and the new social media.

The sport sociology subfield of Olympic studies, with some exceptions, has not arrived at what Australian sociologist R. W. Connell termed the "'ethnographic moment' ... in which the specific and the local are in focus."[7] Sport ethnography was considered an emerging trend in 2002,[8] but, in relation to the Olympics, structural barriers have limited researchers' access to high performance athletes and to the inner workings of the Olympic industry. More ethnographic research would supplement the few biographies and autobiographies that have been published, and would add invaluable depth and insights into the experiences of Olympic athletes with diverse sexual and social identities. I was fortunate to have the opportunity to interview former Olympic swimmer Nikki Dryden, now a human rights lawyer, and her insights and her experiences as a young athlete have added immeasurably to this book.

The secondary sources that I have used cover many fields, including sociology, history, philosophy, social psychology, education, women's studies and cultural studies, leading to an eclectic theoretical approach. All these methodological approaches and bodies of literature are reflected in the following chapters. Because I taught in the area of women's studies from 1986 to 2007, my focus on gender has tended to be a focus on women, but the intersectional analysis used here broadens the scope of the discussion.

My original plans for the organization of the book changed as I began to write. I had divided Olympic history into two convenient periods – from 1896, the year of the first modern Games, to 1936 and from 1948, when they resumed after World War II, until the present. This periodization worked well for some but not all of the themes that I planned to investigate. It soon became apparent that my goal of identifying continuity as well as change required an overview of developments throughout the 20th century and into the 21st rather than an arbitrary division between the two periods. Nor is the discussion of historical themes purely chronological. There are countless examples of issues and controversies that arose in the early 1900s reappearing in slightly different forms to constrain women and disadvantaged minorities throughout the century, and some are recurring in the second decade of the 21st century. The most significant issues have involved the rulings of the IOC and international sport federations, media coverage, societal attitudes

DOI: 10.1057/9781137291158

and the views of so-called experts on sex, gender and sexuality. Equally important, many resistance movements had their beginnings in the first period, and some of the early liberal versus radical debates that arose within these organizations in the early 20th century are still in evidence today.

It will soon become apparent that this book does not attempt to provide a comprehensive history of every Olympic Games, every sport or the experiences of every national team since 1896. There is more extensive discussion of summer sports than winter, and there is more sustained analysis of sports such as track and field, swimming and skating, mainly because of the many controversies over the male and female sporting body that have been played out in these contexts. For a thorough social history of the Olympic Games, sport historian Allen Guttmann's extensive list of publications will answer almost any question.[9] Although I have found his books indispensable, like other sport historians I challenge some of his analyses, but he is not, of course, the only scholar whose interpretations of Olympic history are scrutinized in the following chapters.

Among the secondary sources, in addition to the broad surveys of Olympic history, there are invaluable accounts of individual women and minority athletes, as well as events and themes hidden from history, in the pages of sport history journals and conference proceedings. The biennial International Symposium for Olympic Research held at the University of Western Ontario, Canada, since 1992 offered welcome opportunities for presentations and critical dialogue on these issues. A particularly significant contribution comes from Native Canadian scholar Christine O'Bonsawin, whose work I have cited extensively. There is a dearth of sport-related research written from the "insider" perspective of a minority group, one outcome of the systemic barriers based on gender and ethnicity that operate within the academy.

Writing about the experiences of Olympic athletes outside English-speaking countries presented the usual challenges. As transnational feminists explain, uncritical reliance on secondary sources authored by western scholars risks perpetuating ethnocentric and/or racist assumptions. As a result, some topics are not examined in detail because of a dearth of reliable sources in English, and I have been cautious about citing work by "outsiders."

Another chapter in my original plan would have focused specifically on "the usual suspects," as I termed them: the mass media. I soon realized

DOI: 10.1057/9781137291158

that media coverage of Olympic sport, and the media's contribution to, or generation of, controversies involving women, ethnic minorities and sexual minorities, was an integral part of every chapter, and should not be isolated from the rest of the book. I did not conduct a comprehensive review of the large body of research on media treatment of female Olympic athletes, since this is a particularly well-researched field in sport sociology and communication studies. Content analyses and quantitative surveys of print media are relatively easy to conduct online, and this may be a factor in their popularity. However, some discussions of media coverage present a decontextualized analysis of texts and images, and questions of intersectionality are sometimes overlooked. I found that the integration, rather than separation, of media-related themes provided a more effective means of conducting an intersectional analysis.

In yet another departure from my original outline, I have integrated examples of resistance to Olympic hegemony – the alternative international sporting festivals organized by women, gays and lesbians, workers, Indigenous peoples and other groups – throughout the book, as well as devoting a separate chapter to the topic. By doing so, I make resistance a continuing and salient theme.

Another early inclusion and later omission in the book was the topic of disabled sport and critiques of the Paralympic Games, in the broader context of the politics of disability and the disability rights movements of the past few decades. These important issues merit a book-length discussion of their own. Since by definition achievement sport recruits and rewards the fastest, highest and strongest athletes, the Olympic door is already closed to many people with disabilities. As sociologist Karen DePauw's 1997 analysis shows, the ideal body in Olympic sport is represented by the able-bodied male athlete, thereby marginalizing women and people with disabilities. In this context, Paralympic athletes and the Paralympic Games will inevitably be measured against the so-called real Olympics, a trend reflected in condescending and/or minimal media coverage and limited interest on the part of sponsors. Recent critical research has questioned the extent to which the Paralympics are empowering or disempowering, and to what degree they remain a "freak show." Among many people with disabilities, Paralympic athletes are seen as "super-crips" and are unlikely to be regarded as exemplars.[10] On the other hand, there is ample evidence of the ways that marginalized groups have used sport as a site of resistance, and, as DePauw optimistically concludes, "the cultural transformation of sport is possible."[11]

DOI: 10.1057/9781137291158

As I explain in Chapter 3, it is not my intention to identify social inequalities and then to call for a simple "equal opportunity" solution for Olympic sport programmes, IOC governance and so on. Having said that, I realize that one of the most obvious ways of measuring injustice is to make quantitative comparisons between members of the dominant group (heterosexual, white, middle-class men) and those of the disadvantaged groups (all women, gays and lesbians, working-class people, ethnic minorities and Indigenous peoples). In other words, the dominant group is used as the yardstick by which to measure the progress of the subordinate groups, a liberal approach that is based on the false assumption that the "losers" should simply aspire to catch up with the "winners." And so, although I cite some of these comparative statistics, I try to avoid the implication that numerical parity – a "level playing field" – would achieve the goal of social justice in sport. Instead, throughout the book, I problematize the playing field by questioning whether equal Olympic opportunity would benefit women and disadvantaged groups. My answer is, for the most part, negative.

Gender politics and the Olympic industry

The first two chapters lay the foundation for the subsequent analyses of historical and contemporary trends relating to gender politics. Theoretical insights from cultural studies, critical race studies and sport sociology lead to a discussion of the limits of liberalism, a critique of "equal Olympic opportunity" discourse, and the rationale for an intersectional analysis.

I examine relevant aspects of Nancy Chodorow's work on *being* and *doing* in relation to gender, and Judith Butler's more recent postmodernist analyses of gender and performativity. Research from social psychology on body integration has some important implications for analyses of women and sport, most notably the finding (from western countries) that body image is the major determinant of females' self-image. Then, turning to the work of anti-racist scholars, I present the three key elements of an intersectional analysis – identity construction and the body, symbolic representations and social structures – and discuss their relevance to an analysis of Olympic sport.

On these issues, Henning Eichberg's three-sport model – achievement, fitness and body experience sport – provides a useful framework

DOI: 10.1057/9781137291158

for examining developments over 115 years of Olympic history, and the implications for women and disadvantaged minorities. The growing global power of the Olympic industry has resulted in the sportization of traditional physical recreation, with significant impacts on sporting practices in the western world as well as in developing countries.

Since gender politics and issues related to identity construction and the body are at the centre of this analysis, the literature on historical and contemporary issues directly related to sex and sexuality is particularly relevant. A review of research on "sportsex" and the *eros*/sport connection goes to the core of the gender politics debate, by focusing specifically on the sexualized bodies of male and female athletes.

Chapter 4 examines challenges to Olympic hegemony, beginning in the early 1900s with the Women's Olympics. Some of these early alternative sport festivals continue today; most have direct or indirect connections to national Olympic committees and international sport federations, while a few maintain complete independence. The Gay Games provide an example of an international competition with a combination of achievement, fitness and body experience sports.

The issue of the democratization of sport is further examined by looking at the gender, class and racial/ethnic backgrounds of national teams that participated in the Olympics over the century. Questions of inclusion as well as exclusion are addressed in order to reveal the ways in which athletes, female as well as male, were used in the service of nationalism. On a different aspect of inclusion, I examine the appropriation of Indigenous people's bodies as well as their culture in Olympic ceremonies and promotional materials.

An analysis of a longstanding question in Olympic sport – "Why do they always win?" – demonstrates how sport officials, journalists and scientists in western nations have searched for answers to what they see as the unexpected and unexplained sporting achievements of African and African American athletes, investigations that perpetuate racist stereotypes and racism.

Chapter 5 looks at two sites, the swimming pool and the skating rink, in order to investigate how skaters' and swimmers' bodies are gendered, raced and sexualized. Over the century, swimming and figure skating have seen a number of challenges and changes, some progressive, others that maintain the status quo. In contrast to the heteronormative agenda of Olympic figure skating, the Gay Games programme includes same-sex pairs, and synchronized swimming is open to men as well as women.

DOI: 10.1057/9781137291158

These and other aspects of the Gay Games expose inherent contradictions in the gendered inclusions and exclusions of international sporting competition.

In Chapter 6, I return to the themes of sex and sexualities, mass media sexploitation of Olympic sportswomen and other sex-related issues involving Olympic industry officials in bid and host cities. An analysis of anti-doping campaigns and developments in the IOC's gender verification process since the 1960s provides further evidence of the preoccupation with gender binaries. I continue to analyse homophobia in sport since the 1920s, and the differential impacts on male and female athletes of all sexual orientations. My focus then turns to the issues of prostitution and sex trafficking in Olympic host cities, topics usually hidden from Olympic history. I contrast the priorities of liberal sport feminists who campaigned to have the women's ski jump included in the 2010 Vancouver Olympics with socialist and radical feminists' efforts to protect Vancouver's homeless women and prostitutes, whose safety was further jeopardized by the Olympics. In the concluding chapter, I bring these themes and topics together and look at the potential for resistance offered by the new social media.

Given their 1896 starting date, the modern Olympic Games have a relatively short history. In contrast, women, men and children have engaged in a wide range of physical activities that can be classified as sports since human societies began. Why, then, are certain sports on the Olympic programme, while others are not? Why are some designated as women-only, others as men-only? Why do affluent western countries top the medal tables? Why are some Olympic sports dominated by child athletes, usually girls? Why are some alternative sport festivals successful? Why did some disadvantaged groups organize alternative and autonomous games, while others sought Olympic recognition?

Although there are no simple answers to these questions, the following chapters point to the power and privilege that resides in the IOC as it carries out its self-appointed role as the moral authority for world sport. For their part, many of the Olympic resistance movements focused on the situation of one disadvantaged group rather than recognizing multiple and connected systems of oppression. In the case of women, liberal feminism in the academy and in the sport community worked against the kind of solidarity that would pose a serious challenge to the Olympic industry.

DOI: 10.1057/9781137291158

Notes

1   H. Lenskyj, *Out of Bounds: Women, Sport and Sexuality* (Toronto: Women's Press, 1986).
2   V. Paraschak, Review of H. Lenskyj, *Out of Bounds*, *Sport History Review* 19:1 (1988), 85–8.
3   See, for example, M. Warner, Fear of a Queer Planet, *Social Text* 29 (1991), 3–17.
4   M. McDonald, Beyond the Pale: The Whiteness of Sport Studies and Queer Scholarship, in J. Hargreaves, Ed., *Sport, Sexualities and Queer Theory* (London: Routledge, 2006), 33–45; P. Griffin, *Strong Women, Deep Closets* (Champaign, IL: Human Kinetics, 1998); H. Lenskyj, *Out on the Field: Gender, Sport and Sexualities* (Toronto: Women's Press, 2003).
5   I recognize that the term "race" is not a valid scientific concept, but I have chosen not to put it in quotation marks.
6   H. Lenskyj, *Inside the Olympic Industry: Power, Politics and Activism* (Albany, NY: SUNY Press, 2000), chapter 4. For other publications, see Bibliography.
7   R. W. Connell, Masculinities and Globalization, *Men and Masculinities* 1:1 (1998), 4. One exception is Nancy Theberge's study of the Canadian women's national ice hockey team, *Higher Goals* (Albany, NY: SUNY Press, 2000).
8   R. Sands, *Sport Ethnography* (Champaign, IL: Human Kinetics, 2002).
9   See A. Guttmann's publications in Bibliography.
10   K. DePauw, The (In)visibility of Disability: Cultural Contexts and "Sporting Bodies," *Quest* 49 (1997), 416–30; O. Schantz and K. Gilbert, The Paralympic Movement: Empowerment or Disempowerment for People with Disabilities? In H. Lenskyj and S. Wagg, Eds, *Palgrave Handbook of Olympic Studies* (Basingstoke, UK: Palgrave Macmillan, 2012), 358–80.
11   DePauw, 427.

DOI: 10.1057/9781137291158

2
Beyond Binaries: An Intersectional Analysis

Abstract: *Sex, gender and sexuality are actively constituted and fluid, not biologically predetermined and immutable. Athletes challenge gender binaries by embodying and performing a wider range of femininities and masculinities. The analysis presented here is based on three models of sportive movement, in combination with the key elements of an intersectional approach: identity construction and the body, symbolic representations and social structures.*

Lenskyj, Helen Jefferson. *Gender Politics and the Olympic Industry*. Basingstoke: Palgrave Macmillan, 2013. DOI: 10.1057/9781137291158.

In this chapter, I will review some key works in the fields of feminist theory, social psychology and cultural studies that provide a useful lens through which to examine questions of gender politics and the Olympic industry. These analyses demonstrate how sex, gender and sexuality are actively constituted and fluid, not biologically predetermined and immutable. Thus, it is possible, over time, for female and male athletes to challenge gender binaries by embodying a wider range of femininities and masculinities. To complement this more individualistic perspective, I will develop a critical sociological analysis that examines models of sportive movement, identity construction and the body, symbolic representations and interlocking systems of oppression – that is, an intersectional analysis.

Being and doing/sex and gender

Nancy Chodorow's work linking feminism and psychoanalytic theory was first published in the 1970s and 1980s, the early years of western women's movements, but some key aspects remain relevant.[1] In terms of basic sexual identity, as she explains, the traditional socialization of boys and men in most cultures requires that they establish their masculine identities by *doing*, in order to overcome any sexual ambiguities or insecurities. Girls and women, on the other hand, have a clearly ascribed feminine identity that requires no proving – simply *being* (biologically) female is sufficient – but they are disadvantaged because that identity is undervalued in most societies. In making these claims, Chodorow cites extensive anthropological as well as sociological research.

Chodorow emphasized that she was not proposing a straightforward reversal of this unbalanced "being *versus* doing," and thus challenged liberal feminism's calls for simple equality. Rather, she questioned the underlying assumption that a stable sexual identity was necessary for men or for women, thereby introducing the notion of gender fluidity before it was popularized by cultural studies theorists of the 1980s and 1990s. Furthermore, she argued that the process of *doing* should be "a creative exercise of...humanity" rather than a reaction to insecurity about sexual identity, while the process of *being* should signify positive acceptance of self rather than resignation to inferiority.[2] In other words, she challenged prevailing active/passive and instrumental/expressive sex binaries by calling for processes of sexual identity formation to be purposeful, fluid and inclusive.

DOI: 10.1057/9781137291158

In the sporting arena, as in most areas of social life, males are evaluated first and foremost on the basis of their actions and achievements (what they do), with their appearance and character (who they are) a lesser consideration. A pertinent example involved Australian swimmers Nick D'Arcy and Kenrick Monk, who, shortly before the London 2012 Olympics, put pictures of themselves posing with shotguns and pistols on D'Arcy's Facebook site. This action prompted the Australian Olympic Committee to announce what they apparently considered an appropriate punishment: the two men had to leave the Olympic Village as soon as their events were over, and were prohibited from using social media. They already had reputations as "men behaving badly": D'Arcy had an assault conviction, and Monk had made a false statement to police. Despite these histories, both were selected for the national team. Interestingly, some 50 years earlier, during the 1964 Tokyo Olympics, champion Australian swimmer Dawn Fraser had committed some minor offences: she had marched in the opening ceremony against the coach's orders, and had stolen an Olympic flag as a prank. These actions resulted in her 10-year suspension from the national team.[3]

When women go beyond merely *being* to *doing* – performing in a public arena – they face much harsher scrutiny than their male counterparts on a number of fronts. Their achievements are judged in conjunction with their appearance, personality and lifestyle – that is, the embodiment of a feminine sexual identity – and all these factors influence the final assessment. As the following chapters will demonstrate, there is ample evidence from women's sporting history since the early 20th century to support the claim that a conventionally feminine image trumped athletic achievement if sportswomen hoped to gain public recognition and approval.[4] The pressure to *look* feminine (a code word for heterosexually attractive), regardless of their actual sexual orientation, produced the longstanding phenomenon of the "female apologetic": sportswomen's careful management of appearance and behaviour to offset "unfeminine" athletic prowess and to avoid rumours that they were lesbian.[5]

In the past few decades, women's movements, progressive men's movements and lesbian/gay/bisexual/transgendered (LGBT) movements have in various ways confronted notions of gender-role conformity and heteronormativity. Male athletes face fewer challenges in terms of establishing a heterosexual identity, since most of the physical activities and contests that have come to be defined as *sport* – and included on the Olympic sporting programme – unequivocally confirm hegemonic masculinity

DOI: 10.1057/9781137291158

(with figure skating one of the few exceptions to this trend).[6] For female athletes, however, many of the historical barriers and constraints still apply.

Performativity and gender

Judith Butler's concept of "performativity," as explained in her 1990 publication *Gender Trouble*, challenged the popular interpretation of gender-appropriate acts as expressing a stable identity based on biological sex. Instead, she proposed a different starting point, by suggesting that gender is not merely *expressed* but is *constituted* by the repeated performance of conventional gestures, movements and styles. "Through the repetition of gendered acts, we come to be the gendered self we have learned to perform... within the limits of a small range of viable roles" that are based on cultural norms.[7] This approach challenges the deterministic view of a fixed supply of gender-specific talents and desires waiting to be released and expressed. Rather, it allows for a fluid and ongoing process that offers the potential for resistance through new performances of gender.

In relation to femininity, the concept of performativity may appear at first glance to be incompatible with the seemingly passive notion of *being* (female) that Chodorow advanced. However, the acceptance, as well as the rejection, of a socially prescribed female sexual identity requires the *performance* of selected movements, gestures and styles. For example, learning how to walk is a basic developmental task of early childhood, whereas learning how to walk in high-heeled shoes represents the performance of gendered movements associated with women (and drag queens).

Applied to sporting masculinities and femininities, the idea of performativity as the "stylized repetition" of movement describes the basic components of physical activity. One of the early feminist analyses of women and sport, "Throwing Like a Girl: A Phenomenology of Feminine Body Comportment, Motility and Spatiality," was written by philosopher Iris Young in 1980.[8] The fact that the phrase "throwing like a girl" still resonates more than 30 years later attests to the lasting power of gendered assumptions about movement and athletic performance. In the case of throwing a ball, the repetition that constitutes this *girl* style involves tightly controlled arm and leg movements, underuse of

DOI: 10.1057/9781137291158

physical capacity and the tendency to take up as little space as possible. In contrast, according to this line of reasoning, a girl who throws like an athlete is labelled a tomboy – not a desirable feminine identity. And a female tennis player with an "unbelievably" powerful serve and topspin "plays like a man," according to Dominika Cibulkova in a reference to Samantha Stosur's performance in the 2012 French Open.[9] Significantly, the comment attracted worldwide attention and Cibulkova was pressured to reconsider her statement.

Since the 1960s, the Olympic Games and other international sporting events have become primarily media spectacles, with athletes performing on the world stage through the medium of television. For the duration of the 2008 Beijing Olympics, it was reported that 70 per cent of the world's population watched television coverage.[10] Hence, control over the portrayals of female and male sporting bodies is for the most part in the hands of the western television industry. At the same time, these very public gendered performances also offer a potential challenge to hegemonic femininities and masculinities by revealing how gender categories are fluid and unstable.

As Butler explains, an athlete such as Martina Navratilova generates "a crisis in the category of 'women' as used in the field of 'women's sport,'" by exposing understandings of gender as tenuous and contested.[11] Before the 1950s, western cultural idealizations of female athletes' bodies were relatively close to prevailing norms of femininity. Because training programmes for athletes, male or female, were relatively limited, and scientific applications of strength training had yet to be developed, the physical appearance of female athletes did not change dramatically as a result of their sporting participation. Furthermore, the image of "healthy womanhood" embodied by white sportswomen could always be appropriated as a national icon.

Before the global influence of the mass media, heteronormative ideas and ideals of femininity lay largely in the hands of doctors and physical educators. A moderate amount of physical activity was positively associated with women's health and reproductive capacity, with an emphasis on the crucial links between motherhood and nationhood. To safeguard health and propriety, the first 50 years of the Olympic programme limited women's sports to those that did not pose any (alleged) threat to their uteruses. On the matter of muscles, unsurprisingly, experts agreed that they should be "feminine." If a prominent female athlete was perceived as having "masculine" muscles, she was subjected to public scrutiny

DOI: 10.1057/9781137291158

and censure, and by the 1960s these concerns prompted sex testing in Olympic sport because of suspicions that some female athletes were in fact male (see Chapter 6).

A well-known scene from the 1985 documentary *Pumping Iron II* captures the arbitrary nature of gendered definitions of muscles. A group of elderly white men, judges of a women's bodybuilding championship, are struggling to come up with a definition of "femininity." Affronted by the appearance of "overmuscular" Australian bodybuilder Bev Francis, one judge explains that they are "looking for something that is right down the middle ... a certain amount of aesthetic femininity but yet has the muscle tone to show that she's an athlete."[12] Later in her bodybuilding career, Francis grew her hair long, started wearing makeup and had plastic surgery to reduce the size of her nose. As she explained: "I tried to portray as much femininity as I could in my own context."[13]

As Butler notes, bodies like Navratilova's (and Bev Francis') were initially viewed as "too masculine, even monstrous," but by the end of the 20th century they had become more commonplace – "a new ideal of accomplishment and grace."[14] One can test this theory by looking at images of female bodybuilders from the early 1980s, such as the photograph of Christina Dutkowski in *Out of Bounds*.[15] At the time of the book's publication, the photograph was viewed with surprise and shock, but 25 years later it was much less likely to evoke such a reaction.

While these women's gendered performances gradually produced a new ideal, other women were not so successful. Sexually ambiguous female athletes (often referred to by the controversial labels hermaphrodite or intersexed) largely remain "monstrous" in the eyes of sport officials, the mass media and the viewing public, as the controversy over South African sprinter Caster Semenya has demonstrated (see Chapter 6).

Body integration: am I (only) my body?

On the specific issue of the body, extensive social psychology research, mostly conducted in western countries, has demonstrated that body image is a major factor in determining girls' and women's self-image.[16] The process of self-identification occurs within a context of culturally specific social structures and representations of femaleness generated in the family, school, community and mass media. A 2005 study on gender differences in body dissatisfaction and self-esteem revealed that boys

DOI: 10.1057/9781137291158

and men could "more readily receive self-esteem from other sources, e.g., money, status."[17] Strategies that increased the influence of non-appearance-related sources of self-esteem for overweight girls (and, in fact, for all girls and women) included academic achievement, sporting ability and a pleasant personality.[18] However, in western societies saturated with images of the ideal, ultra-thin female body, girls' and women's capacity to maintain both high self-esteem and high body-esteem is threatened on a daily basis. Several meta-analyses have provided ample evidence that girls' self-esteem dropped during adolescence, and that women's self-esteem was moderately but significantly lower than men's.[19] In short, the statement "I am my body" sums up the identities of significant numbers of girls and women. And if that body does not conform to the criteria of hegemonic femininity (that is, heterosexual attractiveness) because it is an athlete's body, self-esteem is likely to suffer.

In the 1970s and 1980s, confusion between sex-role orientation (conforming to societal norms of femininity and masculinity) and sexual orientation was not helped by the "pop psych" wisdom of the day, generated by sex-role research, that pathologized girls who climbed trees and boys who played with dolls. In relation to sport, this line of research demonstrated a preoccupation with proving that the alleged incompatibility between the role of (feminine) woman and the role of athlete inevitably produced role conflict. Improving on the earlier personality scales based on traditional, bipolar concepts of masculinity and femininity, later versions such as the Bem Sex Role Inventory treated the traits associated with being masculine and with being feminine as socially desirable for *both* sexes. This led to the classifications masculine, feminine, androgynous and undifferentiated. Significantly, sex-role research of the 1980s reported an association between androgyny and high self-esteem, and androgynous personalities were found among groups of high-achieving women, including athletes. Although it was not a big step forward simply to replace the term "femininity" with "androgyny," the more flexible concept of androgyny had some positive impacts on the image question, to the point where the body and the mindset of a successful female athlete began to infiltrate popular culture in western countries. Nike, for example, was quick to appropriate symbols of female athletes' strength, commitment and achievements, as well as the slightly sweaty, moderately muscled female body. Nike co-opted popular discourse as well: a slogan on a Nike T-shirt on sale in 2012 read "MAKING ROLE MODELS SINCE 1972."

DOI: 10.1057/9781137291158

Overall, self-esteem research in social psychology supports the proposition that, for females, body image is the major determinant of global self-esteem. Accomplishments in other realms, such as sport, contribute little to self-esteem unless they actively contribute to making a more desirable (thin, conventionally attractive) female body. Significantly, several American studies reported that Black females had higher levels of body satisfaction and experienced less pressure toward thinness than white females,[20] a finding that I will investigate in relation to sport in a later chapter.

A 2005 study found that even women who worked out regularly exhibited negative body images. On the issue of weight loss, the authors noted the basic contradiction of female body oppression: "women are trying to make themselves smaller and less noticeable (in order to be noticed)." Within this group of active women, the researchers found that, "instead of congratulating themselves for working to stay physically healthy, [they] often think that they should still be thinner ... regular exercise did not correlate with higher self-esteem in this sample of women."[21] At the same time, hegemonic femininity was constituted through the constant repetition of these workout routines. Clearly, the body surveillance project for women is never-ending, and the rules keep changing: big breasts, small breasts, invisible muscles, toned muscles, and so on.

These findings suggest that the levelling of the playing field and the steps towards equal Olympic opportunity resulting from liberal feminist initiatives of the past half-century have had limited impact in the area of body oppression. The intersectional analysis developed in the next section will investigate these problems further.

Putting it all together: an intersectional analysis

The complex question of intersectionality – how gender, race, ethnicity, social class, sexuality and other social identities intersect in and out of sporting contexts – has received relatively little attention among sport scholars, and even less among sport advocates. Early sport sociology texts illustrated the practice of marking social difference by devoting the prerequisite chapters to women, Black people, Native peoples, disabled athletes, gays and lesbians, while the remaining chapters tended to ignore questions of difference and intersectionality. Underlying these arrangements was the implicit assumption that heterosexual men constituted the reference group against which women and minorities

DOI: 10.1057/9781137291158

were to be measured and marked as different. These were not simply *value-neutral* differences to be celebrated, as proponents of liberalism and multiculturalism would suggest. The Olympic industry's "Celebrate Humanity" campaign of 2000, critics argued, was in reality "the global branding of multiculturalism."[22] Using the language of "Olympic values," it ignored different cultures and ethnicities and obscured racist conflicts and exploitation, promoting instead a vision of Olympic universality as race-less, class-less and egalitarian.[23]

A critical sociological approach examines how fundamental social differences among individuals and groups give rise to a corresponding *ism* – sexism, racism, classism, heterosexism, ableism – that maintains existing systems of power and privilege, inclusion and exclusion, both locally and globally. And those with multiple identities experience multiple forms of discrimination. Critical race theorists use the term "interlocking systems of oppression" to encompass the relationships among hierarchical systems, the complex ways in which they rely on each other and, equally important, the futility of challenging one system in isolation from the others.[24] Furthermore, it is necessary to reexamine social categories and to investigate tensions and differences *within* groups as well as *among* groups. Since the 1970s, when Black women and women of colour identified exclusionary practices within the predominantly white, liberal women's movements in western countries, these tensions have been played out repeatedly, in contexts ranging from the pages of academic sports journals to meetings of feminist sport organizations.[25]

Identities, symbols, social structures

Three key dimensions of intersectionality identified by feminist and anti-racist scholars have direct relevance to an analysis of gender politics and the Olympic industry: identity constructions and the body, symbolic representations and social structures.[26] I will discuss these three areas in relation to the three models of sportive movement developed by Henning Eichberg.[27]

Identity constructions and the body

In relation to identity construction, the sporting bodies in question are differentiated by sex, gender, sexuality, social class, race/ethnicity and

DOI: 10.1057/9781137291158

ability. These categories are overlapping and fluid, with the result that multi-layered male and female sporting identities have emerged over the history of the Olympics. With the relatively recent specialization of body types in specific sports – the ectomorphic body in gymnastics, for example – a sport-related selection process also plays a role in identity construction. And while the performance of sport has a significant impact on athletes' bodies and identities, it is also important to recognize how the athletes, as agents themselves, conform to or resist hegemonic sporting identities. These contradictions and tensions are performed in sporting contexts at all levels from community to global, with a range of outcomes.

Literature on the body and society, based largely on the 1960s and 1970s contributions of Bourdieu, Foucault, Goffman and others, points to two key aspects: the *symbolic* body and the *agentic* body. Symbolic representations have generally attracted more scholarly and popular attention than the potential for the body to act as an agent of resistance and transformation, that is, the ways in which "social actors appropriate and manipulate the body's symbolic capacities for their own ends."[28]

The three models of sportive movement that Eichberg developed in a 1998 paper and expanded in 2004 provide a valuable framework for examining sporting identities. Noting that there are numerous models of global sporting practices, he examined the dominance of *achievement sport*, which is at the core of the Olympic faster/higher/stronger ethos. This model focuses on producing quantifiable records, thus leading to an *identity of production*. Marxist scholar Jean-Marie Brohm had developed a similar analysis in 1968, when he examined how dominant forms of sport in bourgeois capitalist industrial society, characterized by competition, maximum output and exploited labour, reflected and reinforced the political unity of those societies.[29] Brohm was citing earlier work by Pierre Laguillaumie, Ginette Berthaud and other French scholars of the 1960s, who in turn may have been influenced by leaders of the international socialist workers' sport movement of the 1920s and 1930s – Julius Deutsch, for example.[30] Socialist influence on English-language sport scholarship was limited until Brohm's book was translated in 1978 and gained wide currency.

From its inception, the IOC has made no secret of its goal of bringing about the "global sportification of physical activities," that is, the diffusion of modern achievement sports to supplant traditional and alternative sports.[31] There is no doubt that this was Coubertin's purpose when,

DOI: 10.1057/9781137291158

in 1923, he proposed holding the first African Games, and famously pronounced "sport will conquer Africa": "a colonization of sport and a colonization by sport," as Suchet et al. expressed it.[32] By the end of the 20th century, however, some Indigenous peoples and citizens of formerly colonized countries were working towards the decolonization of sporting practices, as seen, for example, in the Indigenous games held in Australia, Canada and the United States.[33]

Eichberg's second sport model, *fitness*, promotes the health and wellbeing of all participants – for example, the European gymnastics tradition – leading to an *identity of integration*. Finally, the *body experience* model focuses on dance, play and games, including traditional sport and folk traditions as well as new and emerging expressions of body culture, which lead to a *popular identity*. Eichberg proceeded to examine how the models contribute to the production of national identities: achievement sport and the logic of the market, fitness sport and the logic of the state, and body experience sport and the logic of civil society.[34]

Despite the rhetoric concerning legacies that will benefit local communities and role models who will inspire greater sport involvement, the Olympic industry does not concern itself with fitness and health, or with the development of playful body experience and popular identity.[35] An Australian government survey conducted in the years following the Sydney 2000 Olympics found no increases in community participation in Olympic sports. In fact, non-organized sport and recreation were the most popular kinds of physical activity, and there was significant growth in aerobics and fitness activities.[36] These findings cast serious doubt on claims about the benefits of Olympic legacies and Olympic role models. And, in relation to Eichberg's analysis of links between sporting models and national identities, IOC rules for the conduct of the Games, operating on the logic of the market, actively suppress protesters' freedom of assembly and freedom of speech, both of which are basic requirements for a well-functioning civil society.[37]

Structural changes within the Olympic industry have contributed to the commercialization of sport and the commodification of athletes' bodies. With the 1970s suspension of the amateurism rule and the development of the Top Olympic Partners (TOP) sponsorship programme in 1988, celebrity athletes have increasingly been associated with corporate sponsors and the logic of the market. At the same time, athletes serve the interests of the state, willingly or unwillingly, by embodying national identities. Unsurprisingly, there are occasions when these identities are

DOI: 10.1057/9781137291158

manipulated for nationalist purposes. The 1936 Berlin Olympics are usually cited as the prime example, although there is evidence of these trends in liberal-democratic as well as Fascist countries; as subsequent chapters will demonstrate, nationalism and patriotism are inextricably linked to questions of race and ethnicity.

After the 1988 Seoul Olympics, when Canadian sprinter Ben Johnson tested positive for steroids and was stripped of his gold medal, a cartoon captured his fast-changing, media-controlled national identity: from Canadian sprinter, to Jamaican Canadian athlete and, finally, just Jamaican athlete.[38] Conversely, Olympic victories such as that of Australian Aboriginal runner Cathy Freeman at Sydney 2000 generate "racialized, triumphalist narratives of nationalism."[39] Freeman was packaged as the image of a new era of reconciliation between Black and White Australia, even as the same nation ignored the plight of her people, whose life expectancy in 2000 was close to that of non-Aboriginal Australians about 100 years earlier.[40]

Although there is some overlap between achievement sport, fitness sport and body experience sport, in the most basic terms, as Brohm, Eichberg and others have demonstrated, the achievement model is primarily about work and the experience model is about play. The fitness model encompasses some aspects of both, with recent critiques of "body fascism" demonstrating the (western) fitness sport model's susceptibility to the values and goals of the achievement model and its emphasis on body surveillance and discipline, as well as the obvious relationship to the logic of the market through the fitness industry's financial success.[41]

Symbolic representations

Since the focus of this discussion is the hegemonic embodiments of masculinities and femininities that signify the public face of Olympic athletes, symbolic representations are a central concern. A statement from the public relations firm Hill and Knowlton, employed by the IOC in 1999 to deal with its bribery and corruption scandals, captures the illusory nature of symbols: "Reputation is a state of mind, a set of memories."[42] In the years since the crisis, Hill and Knowlton's efforts – control and manipulation of facts and symbols, including athletes themselves – appear to have succeeded in redeeming the IOC's reputation.

The mass media are largely responsible for the social construction of the lasting images and memories that audiences retain after the Games are over. Selected athletes become the focus of media attention when

DOI: 10.1057/9781137291158

they conform to, or challenge, a specific stereotypical athletic identity – for example, an African American sprinter in the first category, a Muslim sportswoman in the second. These are the men and women who are likely to be selected as subjects of the popular "human interest" or "overcoming adversity" stories prepared for television ahead of the Games. Other athletes who become memorable in Olympic history are those whom the mainstream media target because of anomalies, usually unexpected successes or failures that are subsequently attributed to their gender, race or ethnicity. Another media trope involves the expected failures, again explained in terms of sexist, racist or other prejudicial characterizations of the athletes involved. These mediated images of body + performance play a key role in the gender politics of the Olympics.

Social structures

Finally, the social structures that make up the Olympic industry – the IOC, international sport federations (IFs), national Olympic committees (NOCs) and state or provincial sports governing bodies – represent the fundamental seat of Olympic power.

When Coubertin revived the ancient Olympic Games, he famously pronounced his goal as "exaltation of *male* athleticism," with women's role reduced to spectators and mothers, bearing and raising athletic sons. At the same time, the men's sporting programme upheld a masculine ideal that was compatible with aristocratic gentlemen and military men, whose lifestyles and/or careers allowed them to develop expertise in a number of athletic pursuits, especially those involving running, fighting and weapons. The 1896 men's programme, for example, featured track and field, swimming, wrestling, weightlifting, cycling, fencing, gymnastics, shooting and tennis, and, over the course of the first six Olympics, the number of shooting events for men increased from 7 to 18.

Olympic sportsmen were considered the true *amateurs*; physical education teachers and sport instructors, as well as athletes who received any kind of financial support, were excluded.[43] Even receiving compensation for lost salaries rendered an athlete a professional, according to the IOC's 1930 ruling, which effectively excluded working-class men who could not afford to lose their wages during training and competition.[44] While these amateurism rules upheld the privileged status of male athletes from the middle and upper classes, they also promoted a specific athletic masculinity and masculine body, unmarred by the demands of manual labour. A London coal delivery man, accustomed to lifting

DOI: 10.1057/9781137291158

one-hundredweight bags all day, might have been a contender in the 1896 Olympic weightlifting contest, but he was unlikely to be viewed as a prime example of young British manhood. There were some exceptions to this general trend, with a few policemen, postmen and delivery "boys" from England and Europe among the medal-winners in the first two decades of the century, perhaps giving the appearance of equal opportunity for working-class men.

Sport(ization) for all

The IOC proclaims itself to be "the moral authority for world sport," with an extensive network of overlapping directorships enabling it to fulfil this function. IF presidents and NOC representatives have seats on the IOC, and these are the men, and a few women, who standardize and control every aspect of every sport that appears on the Summer and Winter Olympics programmes, ranging from the approved clothing to the position of the television cameras. For more than a century, the IOC has shaped global sporting practices in accordance with a model of achievement sport that focuses on the competitive production of records, a process that Eichberg and others have terms the "sportization" of physical activities.[45] In other words, the activities that are now defined as sports have been selected from an extensive range of bodily movements, playful pastimes and physical challenges performed by children, women and men globally. Significantly, despite the predominance of the achievement sport model, there are some Olympic events that cannot be judged solely by quantitative assessment. Men's and women's figure skating has been on the Olympic programme since 1908, and events such as ice dancing, trampoline, rhythmic gymnastics (female) and synchronized swimming (female) were added more recently, not without opposition from adherents of the achievement sport model.

Language, power and sport

The popular claim among linguists that language is "a dialect with an army" has some parallels in the global dominance of achievement sport and the Olympic model. Consider the *language* of this model: speed, strength, endurance, competition, teams, records, medals, training, tests, pain, injury, discipline, surveillance, coaches, officials, administrators, sport therapists, sports medicine, sport psychology, rights holders, sponsors,

DOI: 10.1057/9781137291158

stadiums, arenas and so on. In contrast, consider the *dialects* of the subordinated forms of sportive movements, fitness and body experience: play, fun, pleasure, joy, relaxation, reflection, freedom, wellness, creativity, games, festivals, carnivals, dancing, walking, running, skipping, jumping and so on. It is not coincidental that the values implicit in the language of the achievement model, at first glance, suggest male sport, while those of the fitness and body experience models suggest female physical recreation. To the extent that these distinctions are valid, they can be explained as results of socialization, and not in terms of any kind of biological determinism.

It is possible to take these comparisons a step further – into Freudian territory – and consider the links between body experience sport and *eros* (creative life force) on the one hand, and achievement sport and *thanotos* (death force) on the other. Indeed, the "war without weapons" label applied to sports was not merely metaphorical. During the 2011–12 Canadian/American ice hockey season, when the epidemic of concussions among National Hockey League players was finally recognized, more media and public attention was directed at the career-ending impact of head injuries than at their life-threatening potential for the men involved.[46] Clearly, these issues of language and dialect, as I've termed them, reflect and reinforce power relations based on social differences – issues that will be discussed in later chapters.

Sex/gender, the body and sport

In considering gender-related trends in sport, it is useful to consider plural masculinities and plural femininities, in order to reflect the multiple and changing ways they have been defined in different historical periods, cultural contexts and sporting subcultures. An extensive body of sport sociology literature published since the 1980s addresses the ways in which western sporting practices reflect and entrench hegemonic masculinities and femininities – that is, a narrow range of behaviours compatible with common-sense assumptions about the *normal* and *natural* ways of doing gender.

For boys and men, sporting achievements confer status and reinforce heterosexuality, with girls and women, as well as gay men, serving as negative reference groups. Hence, the myth persists that there are no gay men in *real* sports, that is, traditionally masculine sports where strength, endurance and aggression define success. Similarly, the phenomenon of

DOI: 10.1057/9781137291158

men protecting their sport territory from female "intruders" has a long history. The entry of female athletes demystifies and dilutes sport's power to define what it takes to be a man. At the same time, male-only sport provides boys and men with a safe context for physical contact and social and emotional bonding, without necessarily incurring any questions about their heterosexuality.[47] Boys and men whose interests and talents lie in non-traditional physical activities such as figure skating exemplify a less desirable, stigmatized type of masculinity, termed effeminate, sissy or gay.

The IOC has demonstrated a longstanding preoccupation with sex binaries and gender boundaries, paying scant attention to scientific and medical knowledge of the day. Relying selectively on those "experts" whose views were compatible with its rules and practices on sex and gender, the IOC promoted certain privileged forms of femininity and masculinity. The stated purpose of the IOC's sex-testing programme between 1968 and 1998 was to ensure that no male impostors participated in women's events, not to police the boundaries of "femininity." In reality, sex tests under various names (sex checks, sex control, femininity tests, femininity control, gender verification, gender testing) on more than 10,000 female athletes uncovered no male imposters, but identified and disqualified about 27 women with chromosomal and genetic differences that had prompted suspicions that they were not "woman enough"[48] (see Chapter 6).

Sportsex

In one of the most cogent critiques of sport and sex, titled *SportSex*, Toby Miller demonstrates how sports "pick up the body as an icon of difference, coloring it with commercial and cultural referents," commodifying and medicalizing it.[49] He proceeds to examine hegemonic masculinities, commodified and racialized male bodies, lesbian athletes and homophobia. Although Miller portrays the marketing of the sportsex body as emblematic of contemporary capitalism, he identifies its potential for resistance and social change. He explains how recognition of the "physical pleasure and ecstasy" that comes from participating in and watching sport has sparked the reclaiming of public and private health, the critiques of the fast food and tobacco industries and the development of alternatives to competitive sport. The notion of physical pleasure through sport suggests Eichberg's body experience model. "Sportsex" has subversive qualities, in that it challenges the emphasis on standardization and

DOI: 10.1057/9781137291158

quantifiable achievement of Olympic sport, and the medical and social welfare goals of fitness sport.

An important sequel to *SportSex* is David Coad's 2008 book *The Metrosexual: Gender, Sexuality and Sport*. The concept of metrosexuality, characterized by male vanity and narcissism, gained currency in 2002 after an article by British cultural critic Mark Simpson was published on Salon.com. Simpson saw trends in advertising dating back to the 1980s that made men "the object of desire and the male gaze" – thereby establishing the queer connection as well as the new phenomenon of "men as passive sex objects."[50]

The metrosexual identity was soon harnessed by the media and advertisers in the interests of capitalism. Embodied by celebrity athletes such as David Beckham, Michael Jordan and Ian Thorpe, the concept was used to promote sales of high-end consumer brands ranging from men's underwear and skin care products to watches and jewellery. Advertisers quickly disassociated metrosexuality from queerness, and the original, less marketable idea of the male "dandy" evolved to become a heterosexual man who was in touch with his so-called feminine side. Interestingly, these trends did not generate a moral crisis over male power and privilege, presumably because the public faces of metrosexuality had, at first glance, the prerequisite heterosexual credentials, at least in the eyes of the straight world.

Coad's review of developments in western countries produced some interesting contradictory findings: the assumed (and often challenged) association of metrosexuality with homosexuality, professional sportsmen's reluctance to identify publicly as gay, and the fact that "homosocial desire in sport is conducive to the development of metrosexuality."[51]

Talking about *eros*

Discussions of sex and sport based on a feminist analysis are often at risk of appearing puritanical and anti-sex. In an area outside sport, the so-called pornography debates within western feminisms in the 1980s illustrate the dilemma, as one side called for free expression of diverse sexualities in forms ranging from erotica to a woman-controlled sex trade, while the other focused on the direct and indirect harm experienced by girls and women as a result of the sex trade and the pornography industry. In this debate it became clear that one person's *erotica* was another person's *porn*.

DOI: 10.1057/9781137291158

The nude (or semi-nude) calendar phenomenon, a trend that started in 1994 with the Australian women's track and field team, provides a sport-related example. Olympic athletes, in almost all instances women, posed nude for calendars intended to raise funds and lift the profile of their sport. In defence of their actions, the women and their supporters routinely referred to the "tasteful" and "artistic" nature of the photographs and to women's inalienable right to show off their beautiful bodies, while critics identified sexploitation in the same images.[52]

The trend has continued. In December 2011, in the lead-up to the 2012 London Olympics, a British charity published a fund-raising calendar featuring UK Olympic sportswomen: three water polo players, a synchronized swimmer, an artistic gymnast, a kayaker, a triathlete, a runner and a modern pentathlete were photographed wearing expensive lingerie. This may sound like an improvement on the Australian, Canadian and American women's nude calendars to date; however, the black bondage-style lingerie sets, the black stilettos and the "fuck-me" images of seductive, submissive femininity shown in the *Daily Mail Online* were a lot closer to soft porn than the more assertive, powerful and/or playful poses of the nude female athletes in some of the previous calendars. Furthermore, these British women are at the top levels of their sports and yet have almost no visible muscles, thanks (probably) to Photoshop. When I compared the earlier calendars with the 2012 version, I considered revising my former dismissal of the "tasteful" rationale, since that adjective would not describe the lingerie photographs. Ironically, the charity involved was called Wellbeing of Women,

> dedicated to improving the health of women and babies, to make a difference to everybody's lives today and tomorrow. We fund pioneering medical research and training into women's health and use education and information to empower women; so that we can all be at the top of our game.[53]

How the charity's spokesperson (presumably female) could reconcile these images with women's *empowerment* is difficult to imagine.

Sport historian Allen Guttmann bravely confronted the question of *eros* and sport in 1996 in his cultural history *The Erotic in Sport*.[54] Covering 3,000 years of western history, he shows how the Protestant ethic served to suppress the original sexual dimensions of sport in ancient Greece and Rome, until 20th-century developments in the capitalist exploitation of athletes' bodies reversed the trend. In the US, Hollywood began recruiting Olympic celebrities as early as 1932. Their subsequent film

DOI: 10.1057/9781137291158

careers were built on a combination of athletic prowess and (hetero) sexual appeal, with swimmers Johnny Weissmuller, Annette Kellerman and Eleanor Holm and skater Sonja Henie among the earliest examples.

With the so-called sexual revolution in the western world of the 1960s, and the subsequent commercial exploitation of sporting bodies, the sensual pleasures of watching and participating in sport became more explicit and somewhat more acceptable, especially men's enjoyment of female athletes' bodies. And yet, Guttmann claims, the proponents of sport, from physical educators and coaches to sociologists and historians, were quick to deny or decry any erotic elements in sport. It is not fair, however, to attribute these concerns solely to some outdated sense of propriety, when there was ample evidence from historical as well as contemporary trends to show that sexual exploitation, harassment and abuse of female athletes, as well as children and adolescents of both sexes, was a widespread and serious problem. In a climate that normalized exploitative sex/sport connections, the challenges facing the victims and their advocates were often insurmountable.[55]

To the extent that Guttmann validated heterosexual men's enjoyment in watching female athletes in his 1996 book, Brian Pronger's *Arena of Masculinity*, published six years earlier, embraced the erotic aspects of sport for both gay and straight men. As he explained, the appearance of orthodox athletic masculinity in sport – for example, nudity in the locker room – paradoxically disguised its homoerotic possibilities. The vilification of homosexuality was aimed at keeping the homosocial atmosphere of the male locker room unequivocally nonsexual, but it did not always have the intended result, as Pronger amply demonstrates; in fact, a sub-genre of gay male erotica that explicitly sexualized all things sport-related, later referred to as "sporno," has flourished since the 1990s.

When the LGBT web site OutSports.com, established in 1999, presented photo galleries of gay and lesbian athletes in their sporting attire, some observers, including some gay men, were critical of so-called titillating photos that, they claimed, undermined the site's journalistic integrity.[56] OutSports' founders defended the practice by pointing out the double standard: *Sports Illustrated*'s swimsuit issue routinely presented sexualized images for a heterosexual male audience and suffered no threat to its reputation (although they failed to recognize the numerous feminist critiques of the swimsuit issue, as well as of the Australian magazine *Inside Sport* and other similar publications).[57] The title of the relevant

DOI: 10.1057/9781137291158

OutSports Revolution chapter, "It's Not a Gay Thing, It's a Guy Thing," appears to be essentializing gender and mainstreaming gay male desire by establishing common ground with straight men, and the authors refer to studies showing that male arousal is "strongly visual" because men are "inundated with sexual imagery."[58]

The continued popularity of the Gay Games and their growth since 1982, with more athletes participating in the Sydney 2002 Gay Games than in the Olympics two years earlier, demonstrates that the Olympics are *not* the only game in town. Alienated by the homophobia of mainstream sport and the need to conceal their sexuality, these athletes aimed at creating an alternative, inclusive model of sporting competition that welcomed all participants, regardless of sexuality, ability or any other difference. Based on the principles of participation, inclusion and personal best, the Gay Games have no qualification criteria.[59] In the 1990s, however, these principles were diluted by the organizers' move to have Gay Games events sanctioned by international sport federations so that they would serve as qualifying events for the Olympics or other international competitions. In the 1994 Gay Games programme, about one-third of events were sanctioned. Rationales for the change included greater credibility, "a ready-made pool of officials who know how to conduct events" and rule-books that provide structure.[60]

Although some of the early Gay Games organizers said they loved the Olympics – founder Tom Waddell was an Olympic athlete who had remained closeted for most of his athletic career – the separatist ethic of its early years remains strong. Furthermore, there is evidence that it is not so easy to dupe politicized gays and lesbians on Olympic-related issues. In 2010, when a Pride House was set up in Vancouver during the Winter Olympics, its critics pointed to the potential tokenism of this initiative, and challenged the assumption that it signified the acceptance of gays and lesbians in mainstream or Olympic sport. One observer, posting on the web site OutSports, noted that Pride House was organized by a local gay group, not by the IOC or the Vancouver organizing committee, and asked, "So why are we celebrating it? Are you telling me that simply being allowed to have a gay friendly space to co-exist and not forced to shut down, while the Olympics are in the same city, is a victory?" Another post aptly pointed out, "If there had been a Black House for inclusiveness of African-Americans ... after desegregation ... I think it would have been roundly rejected by both Civil Rights leaders at the time and by racists (under another name)."[61]

DOI: 10.1057/9781137291158

Unsurprisingly, Pride House did not attract many openly LGBT Olympic athletes, but organizers claimed that their initial goal was "to open up a dialogue on homophobia in sporting cultures,"[62] not a convincing argument in view of the fact that organizations such as the Canadian Association for the Advancement of Women and Sport and Physical Activity (CAAWS) had opened up this dialogue in the early 1990s.

Why do they always win? Nationalism and racism

Throughout the history of the modern Olympics, countries that consistently produced medallists in a specific sport usually became the focus of public and media attention: Finnish distance runners and British sprinters (male) in the 1920s and 1930s, and Kenyan distance runners (male), African American sprinters and Australian swimmers (male and female) from the 1960s on. If a country produced an unexpected or disproportionate number of winners (according to experts in non-winning countries), questions were invariably raised, the implication being that rules had been broken. (Sometimes they had been, as in the case of East Germany's state-sponsored doping programme; see Chapter 6.)

The existence of a (Protestant) work ethic in combination with genetic good luck was apparently inconceivable if the athletes involved were not white and/or did not come from a (large) western country. Since the 1960s, "scientific racism" has given rise to countless theories about the Kenyans – physiology, genetics, high altitude, climate, diet, hardship and so on – in much the same way that scientists of the 1920s attempted to explain Finnish runners' successes as a result of saunas, diet and links to "a wild Mongolian strain."[63]

In a similar vein, Nazi eugenics gave rise to theories about German athletes' successes, and, more recently, accusations have been levelled at Chinese authorities who allegedly "bred" an exceptionally tall man, Yao Ming, by "encouraging" two very tall former basketball players to marry and forcing their son Yao to play basketball.[64] Yet the question of eugenics was not raised in 2011 when American biotechnology researchers developed genetic tests, available online for direct sale to consumers, to identify the genetic traits in children that predisposed them towards success in a particular sport, although numerous ethical concerns were voiced.[65] Eugenics, it seems, can be associated only with "other" countries.

DOI: 10.1057/9781137291158

Since the 1930s, extensive studies, largely unproductive and usually racist, have attempted to explain African Americans' athletic successes. Following the 1936 Berlin Olympics, American physiologist Charles Snyder examined the correlation between Olympic victories and national populations. Not finding any evidence of Black athletic superiority, he claimed that his scientific method confirmed the athletic superiority of the "great northern nations." He went on to recommend eugenics policies and legislation to preserve "racial purity" and the American way of life, a popular philosophy in 1930s America.[66]

As critics have noted, the mere formulation of any research question that links race and ethnicity to sports performance reflects commitment to a racist ideology.[67] Accounts of the alleged athletic superiority of Black men and women implied, and sometimes stated, that they were "primitive," closer to the animal world, and intellectually inferior. In the US, sportswriters, coaches, doctors, anthropologists, researchers, Black athletes and others weighed in on the question throughout the 20th century, with articles in *Sports Illustrated* and the *Los Angeles Times* clearly having a greater impact on societal attitudes and practices than those in the pages of professional journals.[68] As the debate raged in the 1970s, Harry Edwards, an African American sociologist and former college athlete, successfully challenged the "Black athletic superiority" theory in the popular press as well as in his scholarly books and articles. Answering the unspoken question "Who benefits?" he pointed out that white people had nothing to lose when they supported this idea.

In an era with fewer celebrity athletes and less lucrative career paths in sport, it was true that (alleged) intellectual superiority was a more valuable asset than athletic ability, but by the 21st century, with the globalization of professional sport, the situation was somewhat changed. Summing up the problems in African American communities, Edwards explained, "The dynamics of black sports involvement, and the blind faith of black youths and their families in sport as a prime vehicle of self-realization and social-economic advancement, have combined to generate a complex of critical problems for black society."[69]

African runners, Black winners

As sports geographer John Bale explained in his discussion of Kenyan runners, subtitled "Transgression, Colonial Rhetoric and the Postcolonial Athlete," the appropriation of the Black body was one of

DOI: 10.1057/9781137291158

several forms of colonial textual representation. In the period after their 1960s successes, Kenyans were also subjects of colonial surveillance (measurement of their performance), idealization and naturalization (products of their environment), and denigration ("unfair" victories).[70] The question of African runners' successes remains a magnet for investigative journalists. At the time of writing this (May 8, 2012), I opened the *Guardian Weekly*, a progressive UK newspaper, to see the front page headline "Bejoki, Ethiopia: Why It Turns Out the World's Best Runners."[71] The journalist, Simon Hattenstone, wrote weekly sports columns and feature articles on a variety of popular culture topics. He visited Bejoki, a small town that since the 1990s had produced six world and/or Olympic champion middle- and long-distance runners, women and men, all coached by Sentayehu Eshetu. Predictably, Hattenstone wanted to uncover the reasons for these successes, which Eshetu explained in terms of good diet, good listening and hard work, as well as physical strength from working on the land, lung capacity, optimal body shape and role models. A recent documentary, titled *Town of Runners*, captured the fact that a significant proportion of the town's young population are training as runners.

Nationalism was a key motivator: to honour their homeland of Ethiopia was one of the club's rules, and several athletes mentioned that goal. Significantly, some parents and athletes acknowledged that school-work suffered when intense morning training left children too tired to attend in the afternoon, while others missed school when they left home to go to running camps. According to Hattenstone, "running is a means of escape and transcendence in Ethiopia."[72] Although a few days' visit and a few interviews did not generate enough solid evidence to support this claim, there are possible parallels with African Americans' reliance on sport as a route out of poverty, as Edwards pointed out, a path that is not without significant problems.

On a different ethical question, considerable attention has been directed at the successes of Australian athletes, which have been viewed as disproportionate to population size and attributed to very high levels of government funding. In other words, it seems to be widely accepted that a wealthy country can "buy" medals. According to one cost analysis, "If you want 20 gold medals, then spend [Australian] $800 million every four years."[73] Canadian sport leaders routinely invoke "the Australian model" whenever their own country's medal count is viewed as too low. To acknowledge on the one hand that medal counts are largely dependent

DOI: 10.1057/9781137291158

on a country's wealth, while at the same time embracing Olympic industry rhetoric about fair play, excellence, respect and friendship, would appear hypocritical, to say the least.

Another *Guardian Weekly* article (May 18, 2012) on independent (fee-paying) schools and "public schoolboy dominance" confirmed associations between affluence and success. Although they were only 7 per cent of the population, men who were graduates of these schools were significantly overrepresented in the ranks of media professionals, judges, barristers, academics, business leaders, bankers and even popular culture celebrities and sport figures. Half of the gold medallists at the 2008 Beijing Olympics had received their education in independent schools.[74] Clearly, the playing field is far from flat.

Conclusion

This chapter set out the basic conceptual framework for an intersectional analysis by combining Eichberg's three-sport model with the three key elements of an intersectional analysis: identity construction and the body, symbolic representations and social structures. Drawing on examples from the 115-year history of the Olympic industry, the discussion began the process of decoding themes of gender, class, race/ethnicity and sexuality.

Notes

1   N. Chodorow, *Feminism and Psychoanalytic Theory* (New Haven, CT: Yale University Press, 1989), 23–44.
2   Ibid., 44.
3   Dawn Fraser Still Kicking, *ABC Radio Sunday Profile* (April 15, 2007), http://www.abc.net.au/sundayprofile/stories/s1897086.htm
4   See, for example, S. Cahn, *Coming on Strong: Gender and Sexuality in Twentieth-Century Women's Sport* (Cambridge MA: Harvard University Press, 1994); H. Lenskyj, *Out of Bounds: Women, Sport and Sexuality* (Toronto: Women's Press, 1986).
5   Cahn; Lenskyj, *Out of Bounds*.
6   See Chapter 5.
7   J. Butler, *Gender Trouble: Feminism and the Subversion of Identity* (New York: Routledge, 1990); Butler cited in J. Loxley, *Performativity* (London: Routledge, 2007), 118–19.

8   I. Young, Throwing Like a Girl: A Phenomenology of Feminine Body Comportment, Motility and Spatiality, *Human Studies* 3 (1980), 137–56.

9   Dominika Cibulkova on Sam Stosur, Sports Yahoo web site (June 5, 2012), http://sports.yahoo.com/blogs/tennis-busted-racquet/dominika-cibulkova-sam-stosur-she-played-man-210643207.html

10 Beijing Olympics Draw Largest Ever Global TV Audience, Neilson Ratings web site (September 5, 2008), http://blog.nielsen.com/nielsenwire/media_entertainment/beijing-olympics-draw-largest-ever-global-tv-audience/

11 J. Butler, Athletic Genders, *Stanford Humanities Review* 6:2 (1998), http://www.stanford.edu/group/SHR/6-2/html/butler.html

12 Cited in T. Miller, *SportSex* (Philadelphia, PA: Temple University Press, 2001), 109.

13 Bev Francis quoted in G. Steinem, The Strongest Woman in the World, *New Woman* (July 1994), 71.

14 Butler, Athletic Genders.

15 Lenskyj, *Out of Bounds*, 134.

16 For a fuller discussion, see H. Lenskyj, I Am My Body: Challenge and Change in Girls' Physical and Health Education, in D. Gustafson and L. Goodyear (eds), *Women, Health and Education* (St Johns, NL: Memorial University, 2006), 68–73.

17 M. Tiggemann, Body Dissatisfaction and Adolescent Self-esteem: Prospective Findings, *Body Image* 2 (2005), 129–35.

18 Ibid.

19 L. Groesz, M. Levine, and S. Murnen, The Effect of Experimental Presentation of Thin Media Images on Body Satisfaction: A Meta-analytic Review, *International Journal of Eating Disorders* 31 (2001), 1–16; K. Kling, J. Hyde, C. Showers, and B. Buswell, Gender Differences in Self-esteem: A Meta-analysis, *Psychological Bulletin* 125:4 (1999), 470–500.

20 Kling et al.

21 S. Lowery, S. Robinson, C. Kurplus, E. Blanks, S. Sollenerger, M. Nicpon, and L. Huser, Body Image, Self-esteem, and Health-Related Behaviors among Male and Female First Year College Students, *Journal of College Student Development* 46:6 (2005), 620.

22 M. Giardina, J. Metz, and K. Bunds, USA Celebrate Humanity: Cultural Citizenship and the Global Branding of "Multiculturalism," in H. Lenskyj and S. Wagg (eds), *Palgrave Handbook of Olympic Studies* (Basingstoke, UK: Palgrave Macmillan, 2012), 337–57.

23 J. Maguire, S. Barnard, K. Butler, and P. Golding, Olympic Legacies in the IOC's "Celebrate Humanity" Campaign: Ancient or Modern? *International Journal of the History of Sport* 25:14 (2008), 2041.

24 G. Winker and N. Degele, Intersectionality As Multi-level Analysis: Dealing with Social Inequality, *European Journal of Women's Studies* 18:1 (2011), 51–66;

DOI: 10.1057/9781137291158

P. Hall Collins, *Black Feminist Thought* (New York: Routledge, 1990); M. L. Fellows and S. Razack, The Race to Innocence, *Iowa Journal of Race, Gender and Justice* 1:2 (1998), 335–52.

25 H. Lenskyj, *Out on the Field: Gender, Sport and Sexualities* (Toronto: Women's Press, 2003), chapter 4; M. A. Hall, *The Girl and the Game* (Toronto: University of Toronto Press, 2002).

26 Winker and Degele; K. Crenshaw, Mapping the Margins: Intersectionality, Identity Politics, and Violence against Women of Color, *Stanford Law Review* 43 (1993), 1241–99.

27 H. Eichberg, *Body Cultures* (London: Routledge, 1998); H. Eichberg, The Global, the Popular and the Inter-popular: Olympic Sport between Market, State and Civil Society, in J. Bale and M. Christensen (eds), *Post Olympism? Questioning Sport in the Twenty-first Century* (London: Berg, 2004), 65–80.

28 E. Reischer and K. Koo, The Body Beautiful: Symbolism and Agency in the Social World, *Annual Review of Anthropology* 33 (2004), 308.

29 J.-M. Brohm, *Sport: A Prison of Measured Time*, translated by I. Fraser (London: Ink Links, 1978).

30 See Chapter 3.

31 A. Suchet, D. Jorand, and J. Tuppen, History and Geography of a Forgotten Olympic Project: The Spring Games, *Sport in History* 30:4 (2010), 577; see also D. Chatziefstathiou, I. Henry, E. Theodoraki, and M. Al-Tauqi, Cultural Imperialism and the Diffusion of Olympic Sport in Africa, in N. Crowther, R. Barney, and M. Heine (eds), *Cultural Imperialism in Action: Critiques in the Global Olympic Trust*, Proceedings of the Eighth International Symposium for Olympic Research (London, ON: University of Western Ontario, 2006), 278–92.

32 Suchet et al., 577.

33 Ibid.; T. Miller, G. Lawrence, J. McKay, and D. Rowe, *Globalization and Sport: Playing the World* (London: Sage, 2001), chapter 2.

34 Eichberg, The Global, the Popular and the Inter-popular, 65–71.

35 H. Lenskyj, *Olympic Industry Resistance: Challenging Olympic Power and Propaganda* (Albany, NY: SUNY Press, 2008), chapters 5–6.

36 Independent Sport Panel, *The Future of Sport in Australia* (Canberra: Commonwealth of Australia, 2009).

37 C. Shaw, *Five Ring Circus* (Vancouver: New Society, 2008); C. Zervas, Anti-Olympic Campaigns, in Lenskyj and Wagg, 533–48.

38 Ben Johnson cartoon, originally in *Kingston Whig Standard*; see Miller, *SportSex*, 86–7.

39 Miller et al.

40 Australian Institute of Health and Welfare, *Australia's Health 2000* (Canberra: AIHW, 2000).

DOI: 10.1057/9781137291158

41   B. Pronger, *Body Fascism* (Toronto: University of Toronto Press, 2002).

42   Cited in A. Jennings, Silver Tongues and Olympic Gold, *Sydney Morning Herald* (July 17, 2000).

43   S. Wagg, Tilting at Windmills? Olympic Politics and the Spectre of Amateurism, in Lenskyj and Wagg, 321–37; M. Llewellyn, The Curse of the Shamateur, *International Journal of the History of Sport* 28:5 (2011), 796–816.

44   Llewellyn.

45   Eichberg, *Body Cultures*.

46   P. Goodhart and C. Chataway, *War without Weapons* (London: Allen, 1968); M. Traikos, NHL Misses the Point on Concussions, *National Post* (March 12, 2012), http://sports.nationalpost.com/2012/03/12/michael-traikos-nhl-gms-just-fine-with-status-quo-on-concussions/

47   B. Pronger, *The Arena of Masculinity: Sports, Homosexuality, and the Meaning of Sex* (New York: St Martin's Press, 1990); T. Miller, Commodifying the Male Body, Problematizing "Hegemonic Masculinity"? *Journal of Sport and Social Issues* 22:4 (1998), 431–47.

48   R. James, Genitals to Genes: The History and Biology of Gender Verification in the Olympics, *Canadian Bulletin of Medical History* 28:2 (2011), 339–65.

49   Miller, *SportSex*, 45.

50   D. Coad, *The Metrosexual* (Albany, NY: SUNY Press, 2008).

51   Ibid., 13.

52   Lenskyj, *Olympic Industry Resistance*, chapter 7.

53   M. Rawi, Sporting Calendar Girls! Team GB Model for Charity Shoot ahead of 2012 Olympics, *Daily Mail* (December 22, 2011), http://www.dailymail.co.uk/femail/article-2076668/London-2012-Olympics-Girls-team-GB-model-lingerie-charity-calendar.html

54   A. Guttmann, *The Erotic in Sport* (New York: Columbia University Press, 1996).

55   C. Breckenridge, *Spoilsports* (London: Routledge, 2001).

56   J. Buzinski and C. Zeigler, *The OutSports Revolution* (New York: Alyson, 2007).

57   One of the most extensive and original critiques is Laurel Davis' book *The Swimsuit Issue and Sport* (Albany, NY: SUNY Press, 1997).

58   Buzinski and Zeigler, 41.

59   Lenskyj, *Out on the Field*, chapter 9.

60   J. Clark, Realness … or Sellout? Sanctioned Events in the Gay Games, Joe Clark web site (1994), http://joeclark.org/sanctioning.html

61   OutSports.com discussion board (February 11, 13, 2010), http://www.outsports.com/forums/index.php?showtopic=41887

62   M. L. Adams, *Artistic Impressions: Figure Skating, Masculinity, and the Limits of Sport* (Toronto: University of Toronto Press, 2011), 58.

63   Guttmann, *The Erotic in Sport*, 42–3, quoting Olympic historian John Lucas.

DOI: 10.1057/9781137291158

64 B. Larmer, *Operation Yao Ming* (New York: Gotham Books, 2005).
65 R. Collier, Genetic Tests for Athletic Ability: Science or Snake Oil? *Canadian Medical Association Journal* 184:1 (2011), E43–4.
66 M. Dyreson, From Civil Rights to Scientific Racism: The Variety of Responses to the Berlin Olympics, the Legend of Jesse Owens and the "Race Question," in R. Barney and K. Meier (eds), *Critical Reflections on Olympic Ideology*, Proceedings of the Second International Symposium for Olympic Research (London, ON: University of Western Ontario, 1994), 46–54.
67 S. Fleming and I. McDonald, Racial Science and South Asian and Black Physicality, in B. Carrington (ed.), *Race, Sport and British Society* (London: Routledge, 2001), 113.
68 D. Wiggins, "Great Speed but Little Stamina": The Historical Debate over Black Athletic Superiority, *Journal of Sport History* 16:2 (1989), 158–85.
69 H. Edwards, Crisis of Black Athletes on the Eve of the 21st Century, *Society* 37:3 (2000), 9; see also J. Hoberman, *Darwin's Athletes* (New York: Houghton Mifflin, 1997).
70 J. Bale, Nyandika Maiyoro and Kipchoge Keino: Transgression, Colonial Rhetoric and the Postcolonial Athlete, in D. Andrews and S. Jackson (eds), *Sports Stars: The Cultural Politics of Sporting Celebrity* (London: Routledge, 2001), 218–30.
71 S. Hattenstone, Town of Champions, *Guardian Weekly* (May 4, 2012), 25–7.
72 Ibid., 26.
73 R. Tucker and J. Dugas, What Price for an Olympic Gold? *The Science of Sport* (August 12, 2008), http://www.sportsscientists.com/2008/08/beijing-olympic-medal-price.html
74 J. Sheppard, Gove Decries Public Schoolboy Dominance, *Guardian Weekly* (May 18, 2012), 16.

DOI: 10.1057/9781137291158

3
The Limits of Liberalism: Sex, Gender and Sexualities

Abstract: *Since the 1960s, liberal feminist perspectives have dominated western women's movements, a trend that has prompted radical and minority voices to critique this political approach. If the only women who benefit are white, heterosexual and middle-class, there will be no fundamental challenge to systems of power and privilege based on race and ethnicity, socioeconomic status and sexuality.*

Lenskyj, Helen Jefferson. *Gender Politics and the Olympic Industry*. Basingstoke: Palgrave Macmillan, 2013. DOI: 10.1057/9781137291158.

Since the 1960s, liberal feminist perspectives have dominated women's movements in most western countries, a trend that has prompted radical and minority voices to speak out about the shortcomings of this political approach. In 1979, when Black lesbian feminist Audre Lorde presented her paper "The Master's Tools Will Never Dismantle the Master's House" at a predominantly white women's studies conference in New York, she identified the practice within mainstream feminism of ignoring the voices of poor women, Black and minority women and lesbians. As a result, she pointed out, feminists failed to confront issues of classism, racism and homophobia within the American women's movement.[1] If the only women who benefit from the gains of feminism are white, heterosexual and middle-class, there will be no fundamental challenge to systems of power and privilege based on race and ethnicity, socio-economic status and sexuality.

A few years later, as women made inroads into science and technology, Canadian feminist Ursula Franklin, first female metallurgy professor at the University of Toronto, posed a further challenge to liberalism: "Will women change technology or will technology change women?"[2] In other words, it should not be taken for granted that parity with men will benefit all women, or indeed, any women, much less benefit humanity. At worst, the status quo remains intact and the small number of women who are admitted to male-dominated institutions run the risk of being co-opted. At best, a few pioneering women maintain their commitment to social change, often at great personal cost, as they struggle within the system. Frequently, these women are further burdened with the responsibility of serving as "role models" for girls and young women, a practice that focuses on inspiring by individual example rather than addressing the systemic barriers to women's entry into non-traditional fields.

Liberal routes to equality

Both Lorde's and Franklin's insights can be applied to Olympic sport. History shows that the inclusion of greater numbers of women and other underrepresented groups has done little or nothing to change Olympic sporting practices and the dominance of the faster/higher/stronger sport model. Since the 1960s wave of the women's movement in western countries, women's sport leaders have generally taken the liberal/reform route – a simplistic, additive approach that focuses on removing barriers

DOI: 10.1057/9781137291158

in order to equalize women's involvement. Decades of lobbying the IOC for more Olympic sports and events for women and more women in Olympic governance reflected a liberal preoccupation with simply levelling the playing field, while failing to examine whether it was worthwhile to gain entry to that field, or whether increased female participation would produce unanticipated negative consequences. In light of the fact that the IOC, an unelected group of privileged, predominantly white men, has appointed itself "the moral authority for world sport," it seems unwise to assume that it would be open to the concerns of women and minorities.

Liberal proponents often fail to recognize that western sport priorities are not necessarily the same as those of women or men in countries with different sporting and body-cultural traditions. The right to enjoy a basic level of healthy, pleasurable physical recreation is arguably a higher priority for women globally than the right to equal Olympic opportunity, a right that at best privileges a mere handful of elite athletes. At an international sport sociology conference in the 1990s, I attended a meeting of sport feminists to discuss the formation of an international women's sport organization. Most of these women were recreational athletes with no history of participation in high performance sport. Yet they decided that gender testing in the Olympics would be one of their main priorities, despite my minority view that there were many more pressing and more universal problems that warranted attention.

The Canadian Association for the Advancement of Women and Sport and Physical Activity, founded in 1981, provides a further example of liberal sport feminist organizing.[3] A 2012 post on caaws.ca, for example, provided an uncritical summary of the IOC's 2012 World Conference on Women and Sport in Los Angeles, the fifth such conference since 1996, but the first to which CAAWS had been invited. The major output of the conference was "the Los Angeles Declaration," a set of recommendations that, for the most part, echoed western sport feminists' themes of the past three decades.[4] In contrast, former Olympic swimmer and human rights lawyer Nikki Dryden, who attended as an individual participant, called the conference "a joke." She reported that all the carefully selected speakers gave self-congratulatory presentations, while Olympic officials glossed over difficult issues such as sexual harassment in sport, transparency in Olympic governance and a proposed term limit on IOC membership. Although one panellist, American distance swimmer Diana Nyad, spoke about having been raped by her coach, IOC members did

DOI: 10.1057/9781137291158

not discuss sexual violence in sport at the plenary session. Dryden sat in on the African and Asian regional discussion groups as an observer, and heard those women speaking confidently about the 50 per cent female representation in sport leadership that they had achieved. Then she joined in the North American group's discussion, where a 20 per cent goal was being discussed. Unsurprisingly, the American and Canadian women had assumed that the Asian and African groups were "not as advanced as us."[5]

Transnational feminism serves as a corrective to these liberal approaches by focusing on the central role of colonialism in women's oppression and by incorporating the priorities and initiatives of women's organizations outside western countries. It calls on western feminists to avoid the trap of western superiority and to recognize the problem, and the arrogance, of exporting their specific feminist product to the rest of the world.[6]

An American feminist lawyer recently proposed the kind of culturally insensitive approach that transnational feminists have critiqued when she called on the IOC to impose Title IX on all participating countries in order to "level the Olympic playing field."[7] (Title IX is a 1972 US federal law prohibiting gender discrimination in educational institutions that receive federal funding.) On the basis of the questionable assumption that the IOC is actually working towards "true equality in men's and women's participation," Susannah Carr's article proceeded to tout the successes of Title IX while failing to cite any of its failures. There is an extensive body of research documenting its unintended negative consequences, most notably the dramatic decreases in the number of female coaches and administrators in women's college and university sport. And, although overall female participation has increased, the diversity of sport programmes offered on campuses has been reduced.[8] Even if Title IX had been an unqualified success in the US, that alone would not guarantee its universality. Similarly, as I will argue in Chapter 6, Canadian sport feminists' lobbying and legal efforts during 2006–9 to have women's ski jump included in the Vancouver 2010 Olympics reflect yet another blind sport in white liberal feminism.

The goal of "levelling the Olympic playing field," which has its roots in the American and Canadian women's movements, is not necessarily a high priority for women in developing countries, for women in other western countries or for Black, Indigenous, ethnic minority or working-class women anywhere. Women in developing countries have their own

DOI: 10.1057/9781137291158

critiques of western modernity and their own traditions of resistance, and many distance themselves from western feminist ideas and practices that do not reflect their own realities.[9] Furthermore, even within feminist movements in western countries, there is no consensus regarding the importance of equal Olympic opportunity.

Like many sport feminists in the early 1980s, I joined in lamenting the fact that feminists were generally uninterested in sport issues, while the male-dominated fields of sport sociology and sport history neglected women's issues. However, it soon became apparent that liberal sport feminists' preoccupation with the competitive sport model and the goal of equal Olympic opportunity may have contributed to the lack of interest on the part of non-sport feminists, who tended to dismiss sport as too commercialized, competitive, male-dominated and unlikely to change. When American feminist pioneer Gloria Steinem was writing about her interview with Australian bodybuilder Bev Francis in 1994, she acknowledged her own longstanding anti-sport bias, a rare admission of mind/body dualism in (non-sport) feminist circles:

> I thought of my own years of fierce pride in spurning sport...I became angry for and at myself, one of the countless women who'd gone along with society's denial that we might find any delight in physical daring. How much of the world had I missed while living in my head?[10]

With non-sport feminists tending to "live in their heads" and sport feminists single-mindedly pursuing the liberal route to equality, there were few possibilities for challenging the status quo in Olympic sport.

Equal Olympic opportunity for women: a low bar

Gender parity has long been western sport feminists' main goal: more Olympic sports and events for women, more comprehensive and unbiased media coverage, greater financial support, more sponsorship, better career paths and so on.[11] These strategies fail to address the fundamental flaws in sporting systems, locally, nationally and internationally: the ways in which sport serves to entrench global systems of colonialism and oppression that extend well beyond gender issues. With a focus on western countries, a liberal approach tends to conceptualize a universal "woman" whose athletic talent and commitment deserve full recognition on the world stage, that is, in the Olympic Games. From this perspective,

DOI: 10.1057/9781137291158

the "firsts" take on great significance – the first Muslim woman or the first Aboriginal woman in the Olympics – as if one breakthrough constitutes a landslide victory.

Documenting developments of the 20th century and into the 21st, liberal accounts routinely conclude that the overall treatment of female athletes has been unfair, and that it is high time that the IOC rectified the problem. No reasonable person would dispute this, but it is not my purpose here to lament the fact that the IOC does not treat female athletes and female sport in the same way that it treats male athletes and male sport. From my perspective, this is an unduly low standard. More importantly, it is based on two flawed assumptions: first, that the Olympic industry and sport systems are fundamentally sound, only requiring minor adjustments ("reforms"); second, that what is good for western women and men is good for all women and men. And, on a global scale, it cannot be assumed that the Olympic industry's treatment of white male athletes from western countries constitutes the optimal standard. Although close to half of the positions on the IOC are occupied by white males who might be expected to protect the interests of other white males (athletes), the big financial questions of television contracts and corporate sponsorships have a higher priority than the welfare of athletes, regardless of their gender or origin. From the Olympic industry's perspective, athletes' primary purpose is to provide the means of delivering global audiences to sponsors' products through the medium of television. The one athlete-related issue that commands IOC attention is that of performance-enhancing drugs, with both fairness and health cited as key concerns,[12] but relatively little attention is paid to the equally serious problems that threaten high performance athletes' health and wellbeing, ranging from negligence and abuse of child athletes to brutal training regimens to which athletes of all ages are subjected.[13]

Winners and losers

Following the approach of women in sport leadership, or in some instances taking a leadership role themselves through consulting with governments on sport policy, western feminist academics have tended towards liberal approaches. More than four decades of research and writing has documented a long list of inequalities when measured against the male yardstick, and has called for reform to close the gap between women and men in sport. Extensive analyses of mainstream

DOI: 10.1057/9781137291158

media coverage and advertising images of Olympic sportswomen have clearly demonstrated omissions and distortions, specifically the pattern of trivializing women's achievements and hypersexualizing their bodies.[14] Comparisons with the treatment of male Olympic athletes have often been invoked to demonstrate sex discrimination, the implication being that if only journalists and advertisers would treat women in the same way that they treat men, all would be well. Until recently, media analyses failed to recognize that discriminatory practices, most notably racism and homophobia, can be found in the coverage of male athletes, and that "catching up with the men" does not necessarily signify progress. *Image* is central to the advertising and television industries, and the place of beauty, which I define as conventional heterosexual attractiveness, cannot be ignored. When cameras zoom in on beautiful male as well as beautiful female bodies, and ignore the others, factors beyond sexism are at work. When the bodies of Black men are the main focus, racist commodification is likely to be a factor.

Developments in Canadian and American women's sport advocacy groups demonstrate some of the pitfalls of liberal strategies. CAAWS, for example, was dependent on funding from government agencies, an arrangement that eventually threatened its continued autonomy, and in 1991 it became the equivalent of a government agency. A multi-sport organization at one time housed in the same office tower as other Canadian national sport and multi-sport organizations, CAAWS rose symbolically as well as literally above its humble beginnings in rented space in an old house alongside other feminist groups. As I commented at the time, this was the equivalent of the Canadian Advisory Council on the Status of Women relocating to Parliament Hill.

In the US, the Women's Sport Foundation (WSF) was established by professional tennis player Billy Jean King in 1974, and from 1992 to 2007 its executive director was Donna Lopiano. A comparison of Lopiano's 1984 feminist analysis of women's intercollegiate sport and her 1997 presentation to the annual WSF conference shows a dramatic shift in her feminist political stance. In the earlier article, commenting on the 1981 takeover of the Association for Intercollegiate Athletics for Women by the (men's) National Collegiate Athletic Association (NCAA), she emphasized the importance of taking a radical feminist perspective. Calling liberal/reform approaches "necessary but not primary," she unequivocally denounced the value system of men's sport and its focus on "the economic value of the athlete."[15]

DOI: 10.1057/9781137291158

Thirteen years later, in her role as WSF director, Lopiano discussed the "women's sport explosion," specifically the dramatic increases in American girls' and women's sporting participation and winning performances in the 1996 Atlanta Olympics. Most of her presentation, however, implicitly supported the profit motive. She gave a list of market-related examples, including the untapped women's sporting goods market (and women's "shopping gene"), "NBC's success/Olympic marketing to women," "loyalty marketing to women," "champion female athlete product endorsement," the "feminization of [sport-related] corporate culture" and the "explosion of women's [sport] product" – all a far cry from her earlier critique of the male sport model.[16]

New sports, old attitudes

Liberal lobbying strategies have produced some gains and some losses for women. For example, the introduction into the Olympic programme of women's volleyball in 1964 and women's basketball in 1976 marked the end of more than half a century of Olympiads that had offered no team sports for women. Proponents of other sports had also been lobbying for their inclusion in the women's programme. In 1972, adopting a strategy that at best may have been pragmatic, although it was certainly not progressive, the president of the international rowing federation used the image of "feminine" Dutch sculler Ingrid Dusseldorp, described as having "fantastic legs and a beautiful figure and long fair hair," to persuade the IOC that successful female rowers were not "ugly" or "masculinized" women.[17] Around the same time, the US campaign to have a women's Olympic marathon was based less on radical activism than on the argument that female marathoners were "feminine" as well as athletic.[18]

During the 1980s and 1990s, field hockey (1980), soccer and softball (1996) and ice hockey (1998) were added to the list of women's team sports. As if to balance the scales, the IOC introduced the female-only sports of synchronized swimming and rhythmic gymnastics in 1984, both of which unequivocally reinforced hegemonic femininity. Despite the genuine athletic ability required in all these sports, the superficial image was one of smiling faces and graceful bodies in revealing clothing, with appearance counting as much as performance. The 1996 addition of women's beach volleyball arguably contributed more to the sexploitation of female athletes in sport bikinis than to the advancement of women's sport.

DOI: 10.1057/9781137291158

While the uniforms for team sports largely concealed female bodies and directed spectators' attention to the game, gymnasts', swimmers' and beach volleyball players' attire did the opposite, positioning them solidly in front of the male gaze. Unsurprisingly, only a few years passed before other (mostly male) policy-makers in national women's sport organizations began to eye tighter uniforms for women who played team sports, with Australia having the dubious distinction of being the first to require body-suits of form-fitting Lycra, which in 1998 became the required uniform for women in basketball, netball, volleyball, softball and field hockey.[19]

There are numerous examples of this trend. In 2004, FIFA president Sepp Blatter called for female soccer players to wear "tighter" shorts to increase the game's popularity: "'I Want Short Shorts': Blatter," in the words of one newspaper headline.[20] The Badminton World Federation ruled that women should wear shorter skirts "to boost the sport's profile among viewers and sponsors," and beach volleyball required women to wear sport bikinis, while men wore knee-length shorts and tank tops.[21] The International Volleyball Federation (FIVB) changed this rule in time for the 2012 London Olympics, with a British newspaper proclaiming, "Female Volleyball Players *Permitted* to Wear Less Revealing Uniforms" (emphasis added), an ironic headline in view of the long history of societal constraints on sportswomen's allegedly *over*-revealing uniforms. The new dress code allowed shorts and a sleeved or sleeveless top, on the grounds that many of the countries now participating had "religious and cultural requirements so the uniform needed to be more flexible."[22] In 2010, the FIVB had introduced new Olympic qualifying events – Continental Cups on five continents – to provide countries with more opportunities to compete in the 2012 Olympics, resulting in more women from Islamic countries likely to qualify. Presumably, the FIVB was also aware of the 2012 campaign to encourage and/or pressure Saudi Arabia and other Islamic countries to send women to the London Olympics, and a dress code that hindered those efforts was not conducive to good PR. In the past, Islamic women had competed in other Olympic events wearing more traditional clothing and hijabs, while a few had worn shorts and sleeved shirts, although not without repercussions from conservative sectors when they returned home. And, while western feminists applauded the participation of Islamic sportswomen, they were mostly silent on the question of possible disadvantages posed by clothing that exposed only the hands and the face. In speed events, where every ounce of clothing and footwear is seen as significant, the playing field was far from level.

DOI: 10.1057/9781137291158

Human Rights Watch (HRW) was a key force in the 2012 campaign. It published a report titled "Steps of the Devil," a reference to the conservative religious position in Islamic countries that viewed female participation in any sport or physical activity as the route to immorality. The report noted that prohibitions against female sport were merely one component of a long list of "systemic violations of women's and girls' rights" entrenched through the practice of male guardianship.[23] HRW no doubt selected female sport for its leverage potential in an Olympic year, a worthwhile strategy in itself, and HRW spokespeople pointed out that the overarching problem was these countries' policies barring girls' access to physical education in the schools. However, the global public attention that the campaign generated may have inadvertently conveyed the message that a few Saudi sportswomen at the Olympics would signify a change in societal attitudes and policies affecting all Saudi women.

Women in the boxing ring

In other developments in the lead-up to the 2012 Games, the International Amateur Boxing Federation joined the trend of "feminizing" non-traditional female athletes, by proposing that female boxers should wear skirts. This was the first time that women's boxing had appeared on the Olympic programme. One of the federation's least persuasive rationales was the need to ensure that the spectators could differentiate female from male boxers – evidence of male sport leaders' longstanding preoccupation with gender binaries.[24] These kinds of clothing directives were not universally condemned. Some women asserted that they were comfortable wearing the required attire and were proud of their bodies, as if to suggest that the women who did object were insecure.[25]

In another example of Olympic advertising, CoverGirl cosmetics company selected two boxers, an American and a Canadian, as well as an American beach volleyball player, to feature in their 2012 campaign titled "Anyone Can Be a Model." Conveniently covering several bases at the same time, the company chose a Hispanic American, a Native Canadian and a blonde Californian. This was an astute marketing strategy to capitalize on the novelty of women's boxing, and yet another instance of exploitation of female athletes' bodies. Beach volleyball player Jennifer Kessy claimed it was "the best feeling ever" to be identified as a CoverGirl in magazine ads, a strange admission for an internationally successful athlete heading for the next Olympics. She went on to say, "We are athletes and in turn we are the everyday women ... beauty and

DOI: 10.1057/9781137291158

femininity can come in so many forms" – perhaps a reference to the fact
that the two boxers weren't tall and blonde.

Conclusion

Having identified the limitations of western sport feminists' and sport
scholars' liberal approaches, and the Olympic industry's entrenched
preoccupation with "feminizing" women's sport, I now address the
topic of resistance – the challenges to Olympic industry hegemony
mounted by women and minorities throughout the 20th century and
into the 21st.

Notes

1   A. Lorde, The Master's Tools Will Never Dismantle the Master's House, in
    Sister Outsider (Santa Cruz, CA: Crossing Press, 1984), 110–13.
2   U. Franklin, Will Women Change Technology or Will Technology Change
    Women? *CRIAW Papers* (Ottawa: CRIAW, 1985).
3   For a discussion of developments in CAAWS prior to 1990, see H. Lenskyj,
    Out on the Field: Gender, Sport and Sexualities (Toronto: Women's Press, 2003),
    chapter 4.
4   CAAWS Presents at the IOC Women and Sport Conference (March
    21, 2012), CAAWS web site. http://www.caaws.ca/e/archives/article.
    cfm?id=4451&search=olympic; IOC, 5th World Conference on Women
    and Sport (Los Angeles, CA, February 16–18, 2012), http://www.olympic.
    org/Documents/Commissions_PDFfiles/women_and_sport/Los-Angeles-
    Declaration-2012.pdf
5   Interview with Nikki Dryden (Toronto, May 14, 2012).
6   K. Davis, *The Making of Our Bodies Ourselves: How Feminism Travels across
    Borders* (Durham, NC: Duke University Press. 2007); see also R. Giulianotti,
    Human Rights, Globalization and Sentimental Education: The Case of Sport,
    Sport in Society 7:3 (2004), 355–69.
7   S. Carr, Title IX: An Opportunity to Level the Olympic Playing Field, *Seton
    Hall Journal of Sports and Entertainment Law* 19 (2009), 149–80.
8   See, for example, L. Carpenter and R. Acosta, *Title IX* (Champaign, IL:
    Human Kinetics, 2005).
9   Davis, *The Making of Our Bodies Ourselves*, 72.
10 G. Steinem, The Strongest Woman in the World, *New Woman* (July 1994),
    69–73.

DOI: 10.1057/9781137291158

11   Of the numerous examples, here are some from the UK, the US, and
      Australia: A. Blue, *Faster, Higher, Further: Women's Triumphs and Disasters at
      the Olympics* (London: Virago, 1988); A. DeFranz, The Olympic Games: Our
      Birthright to Sport, in G. Cohen (ed.), *Women in Sport: Issues and Controversies*
      (Newbury Park, CA: Sage, 1993), 185–92; M. Stell, *Half the Race: A History of
      Australian Women in Sport* (Sydney: Angus & Robertson, 1991), 101–39.
12   R. Pound, *Inside Dope* (Mississauga, ON: Wiley, 2006).
13   See, for example, C. Breckenridge, *Spoilsports* (London: Routledge, 2001);
      Lenskyj, *Out on the Field*, chapter 2; J. Ryan, *Little Girls in Pretty Boxes:
      The Making and Breaking of Elite Gymnasts and Figure Skaters* (New York:
      Doubleday, 1995); P. Close, D. Askew, and X. Xin, *The Beijing Olympiad* (New
      York: Routledge, 2007), 170–3.
14   See, for example, N. Rivenburgh, The Olympic Games: Twenty-First Century
      Challenges As a Global Media Event, *Culture, Sport, Society* 5:3 (2002), 31–50;
      G. Daddario and B. Wigley, Gender Marking and Racial Stereotyping at the
      2004 Athens Games, *Journal of Sports Media* 2:1 (2007), 31–51.
15   D. Lopiano, A Political Analysis of the Possibility of Impact Alternatives for
      the Accomplishment of Feminist Objectives within American Intercollegiate
      Sport, *Arena Review* 8:2 (1984), 49.
16   D. Lopiano, Tomorrow in Women's Sport: Now Is Just the Tip of the Iceberg,
      presentation to the annual national conference of the Women's Sport
      Foundation (Bloomingdale, IL: May 17, 1997).
17   A. Schweinbenz and A. Cronk, Femininity Control at the Olympic Games,
      Third Space 9:2 (2010), http://www.thirdspace.ca/journal/article/view/
      schweinbenzcronk
18   A. Jutel, "Thou Dost Run As in Flotation": Femininity, Reassurance and the
      Emergence of the Women's Marathon, *International Journal of the History of
      Sport* 20:3 (2003), 17–36.
19   S. Hughson, The Bodysuit: Empowering or Objectifying Australia's Elite
      Women Athletes? unpublished paper (Canberra: Psychology Department,
      Australian Institute of Sport, 1998).
20   N. Da Costa, "I Want Short Shorts": Blatter, *Toronto Star* (January 17, 2004).
21   Badminton example cited in M. Talbot, The Role of Olympic Education in
      Today's Sport World, presentation to the International Olympic Academy
      (Athens, May 15, 2011).
22   Female Beach Volleyball Players Permitted to Wear Less Revealing Uniforms,
      The Telegraph (March 27, 2012), http://www.telegraph.co.uk/sport/olympics/
      volleyball/9169429/London-2012-Olympics-female-beach-volleyball-players-
      permitted-to-wear-less-revealing-uniforms.html
23   Human Rights Watch, "Steps of the Devil": Denial of Women and Girls'
      Right to Sport in Saudi Arabia (Human Rights Watch web site, 2012), http://
      www.hrw.org/sites/default/files/reports/saudi0212webwcover.pdf

DOI: 10.1057/9781137291158

24 Olympic Boxing Authority to Discuss Women Wearing Skirts, *TSN* (November 4, 2011), http://www.huffingtonpost.ca/2011/11/04/olympic-boxing-authority-_n_1076510.html

25 H. Lenskyj, *Olympic Industry Resistance: Challenging Olympic Power and Propaganda* (Albany, NY: SUNY Press, 2008), chapter 7.

DOI: 10.1057/9781137291158

4

Challenges to the Olympic Industry

Abstract: *Discrimination based on gender, sexuality, class, race and ethnicity, together with the "beauty and grace" prerequisite for female athletes, characterized Olympic sport throughout the 20th century and persists in various forms today. In the face of the Olympic industry's selective inclusions and exclusions, several marginalized groups challenged Olympic industry hegemony by organizing alternative international sport competitions, with varying degrees of success.*

Lenskyj, Helen Jefferson. *Gender Politics and the Olympic Industry.* Basingstoke: Palgrave Macmillan, 2013. DOI: 10.1057/9781137291158.

DOI: 10.1057/9781137291158

The Olympic Games of 1896 to 1936 were conducted during a period of international tensions and upheaval, leading up to two world wars and the rise of Fascism and Nazism in Europe. The same era saw the beginnings of women's and minority rights movements in a number of Olympic member countries. When the Games resumed in 1948, following World War II, it was in a greatly changed political context marked by decolonization and the early stages of globalization. On the social justice front, the 1960s saw a number of campaigns promoting the rights of women and disadvantaged minorities: the civil rights movement in the US, the anti-Apartheid movement in South Africa, Indigenous people's rights in Canada, the US and Australia, and the rights of women, disabled people, and lesbians and gays in most western countries.[1]

In the first half of the 20th century, most Olympic protests and boycotts were prompted by national and international political crises associated with the two world wars. Rather than using the sporting event itself as a platform for political protest, several groups whose members were discriminated against or excluded from the Olympics organized independent games. In the Cold War era, as in earlier decades of the century, political leaders rather than sport leaders initiated protest actions, most notably the boycott of the 1980 Moscow Games by several western countries following the Soviet invasion of Afghanistan. It was not until later in the 1980s that the devastating impacts of the Olympics on vulnerable populations in host cities and countries became more widely recognized, which ultimately led to an international network of community-based anti-Olympic and Olympic watchdog groups. Again, Olympic sport itself was not the target, and Olympic athletes were rarely at the forefront of the protest movements until the IOC crisis of 1998–9. In the wake of the bribery and corruption scandals, a group of current and former Olympic athletes convened an organization known as OATH (Olympic Advocates Together Honorably). They called for democratic IOC governance and the restoration of Olympic ideals, as reflected in the theme of their first symposium, "Ignite the Democratic Flame." As subsequent events demonstrate, steps towards democratization have been minimal.[2]

Alternative (Olympic) games

During the course of the 20th century, a number of international, multi-sport events were organized as a challenge to Olympic sport hegemony. These included the Women's Olympics, Workers' Games,

DOI: 10.1057/9781137291158

People's Olympiad, Maccabiah Games (Jewish), African Games, Games of the New Emerging Forces (Indonesia), North American Indigenous Games, Gay Olympics and EuroGames.³ Some of these games had direct or indirect connections to the IOC, in that they followed a similar model of regional and/or international sporting competition. Some sought and were granted official standing with the IOC and international sport federations, and some were organized by national Olympic committees. Others stood firm as independent alternatives to the games they characterized as the "Bourgeois Olympics" or the "Straight Olympics." The Women's Games and the Gay Games even dared, in their early days, to use the word "Olympic," until the Olympic industry took steps, either behind the scenes or in the courts, to protect its lucrative brand name and preserve its monopoly over world sport. (The Workers' Olympics' use of the "O" word appears to have escaped IOC attention during these games' 12-year history.) At the same time, the IOC, international sporting federations and national Olympic committees took note of changing societal attitudes and the possible financial and public relations benefits of changing with the times, even though they did so at a glacial speed.

Independent games offered opportunities for international competition to groups whose members were marginalized by or excluded from the Olympics because of the elitist nature and limitations of the Olympic programme, the eligibility requirements and the generally chilly climate faced by women, ethnic minorities, working-class people, sexual minorities and others. These games often include non-Olympic sports, as well as folk games and traditional sports that are more reflective of fitness and body expression than the achievement sport model. European gymnastics, for example, are a key component of the Workers' Olympics and the Maccabiah Games, while the Canadian Inuit people's Northern Games offer traditional activities such as the blanket toss, as well as individual tests of balance, power and endurance. Adopting a more relaxed and playful approach to the entire enterprise, the Gay Games (1982), EuroGames (1992) and other LGBT sport festivals include ballroom dancing, bowling, roller-blading, aerobics, hiking and men's cheerleading.

Challenging the Bourgeois Olympics

When the participants shared a political identity – as workers or Indigenous peoples, for example – these events, unlike the Olympics,

DOI: 10.1057/9781137291158

did not generate international rivalries or nationalistic fervour. On the contrary, the four International Workers' Olympic Games organized in Europe by the Socialist Workers' Sport International between 1925 and 1937 were an explicit challenge to bourgeois sport and bourgeois values, rejecting nationalism, capitalism and militarism, and promoting workers' internationalism, class solidarity and peace.[4] There were no entry restrictions based on ability; records were kept, but record-breaking was not the aim of the event. Like the Women's Games, the Workers' Olympics enjoyed considerable success, often attracting much larger numbers of athletes and spectators than the Olympics.

As early as 1928, prominent Austrian workers' sport leader Julius Deutsch labelled as hypocrisy the bourgeois (and IOC) claim that sport must be free from political influence. "It is not true that bourgeois sport is neutral," he explained, because it is "an element in that social order and those cultural notions, which is the historical task and moral obligation of the working class to destroy."[5] Socialist sport leaders in Europe took a stand against the growing competitiveness, brutality and violence in sport, to the point of debating at the 1929 congress whether the rules of (men's) soccer should be changed to reward "aesthetic and fair play."[6] They concluded, pragmatically, that competitive sports, if treated appropriately, would attract young workers into the socialist movement. At the same time, workers' sports organizations aimed at the "democratization" of physical activity and the mass participation of women, men and children, recognizing the financial barriers that workers and their families faced in accessing physical recreation.

On the issue of professional sport, Deutsch was ahead of his time in identifying these athletes' limitations. While he respected sportspeople who earned an honest living, he rejected the concept of the professional athlete as role model: "his or her achievements resulted from exceptional physical characteristics and specialized training ... this special training was not desirable for everybody, because most professional athletes developed some muscles at the expense of others."[7] Throughout the 20th century and into the 21st, critics of the Olympic sport model continued to restate this unpopular position, supported by a growing body of scientific and pedagogical evidence.[8] In 2012, for example, South African sport scientist Tim Noakes argued that top athletes are by definition "genetic freaks"; "that's the whole point of [high performance] sport," he said.[9]

By the late 19th century, the General Jewish Workers' Union, the Bund, was flourishing in Lithuania, Poland, Germany and Russia,

DOI: 10.1057/9781137291158

with workers' sport organizations forming a significant component of the movement, which continued until the Holocaust. As historian Roni Gechtman explained, these working women and men "did not need to prove their muscular and physical skills to counteract a certain abstract conception of Jews as spiritual or intellectual persons. As workers, they were routinely engaged in physical work in any case."[10] Gender differentiation was less rigid in working-class communities: Jewish women, employed outside the home, were expected to be robust and strong, while men could be emotionally expressive.[11] However, anti-Semitism continued to find expression in longstanding and degrading stereotypes of the alleged "defective masculinity" of Jewish men. Historian George Eisen has argued that Olympic sport and ideology provided a means of "psychological and social acceptance" for the growing Jewish middle class in Europe and the US.[12] The emergence of Zionism from the late 1800s was a key factor, as Eisen explained:

> the Bund attempted to adjust Jewish ethics and values to the precepts of Marxism while Zionism attempted to introduce a whole new nationalistic value system. Zionist preoccupation with the body, exercise, and later the Jewish Olympic idea (Maccabiah Games) was a direct consequence of industrialization, urbanization, and anti-Semitic pressures.[13]

There are some clear parallels with other early alternative sport movements, such as the Women's Games, that eventually changed course and followed the Olympic model. First held in 1932, the Maccabiah Games, an international Jewish multi-sport competition, attracted 300 athletes from 16 countries, and the Games have been conducted every four years since the end of World War II. In 1960, the Maccabi World Union (MCU) was designated an "Organization of Olympic Standing" and the Games were "recognized as a Regional Sport Event under the auspices and *supervision* of the International Olympic Committee and International Sports Federations" (emphasis added).[14]

A 1962 letter from the MCU chairman, Pierre Gildesgames, to the IOC, published in *Olympic Review*, revealed some tensions between the two organizations. Gildesgames refuted allegations that the Maccabiah Games discriminated on the grounds of nationality, race and religion. He also reminded the IOC that the Mediterranean Games, held under IOC auspices, barred Israelis and some Jews from participating, and

DOI: 10.1057/9781137291158

he strongly urged the IOC to put more effort into stopping these discriminatory practices. Predictably, the *Olympic Review* editor added his own note in defence of the IOC: "in spite of the fact that it gives patronage to some Regional Games, [the IOC] does not interfere in the internal organization of such Games, providing that they are conducted in accordance with the minimum requirements."[15] Similarly, since at least 1936, the IOC has not "interfered" in the domestic politics of host countries unless it has suited Olympic industry purposes to do so.

The politicizing of sport through workers' sport organizations had significant implications in Europe and beyond. The 1936 Workers' Olympics, scheduled to take place in Barcelona, were organized in protest against the IOC's collaboration with Nazi Germany, evident in its selection of Berlin as site of the 1936 Olympics despite widespread objections. Barcelona had unsuccessfully bid for the same Olympics, and Spain's Republican government called for all international athletes to boycott Berlin and instead participate in the Workers' Games.

In the US, a number of Jewish and labour groups as well as the American Civil Liberties Union led the boycott efforts, which ultimately failed. The openly anti-Semitic and racist American Olympic Committee president Avery Brundage and US IOC member Charles Sherrill reached an agreement with Hitler and the Berlin organizers, and the US team, including Black and Jewish athletes, competed in Berlin.[16] Athletes from 22 countries had planned to attend the Workers' Games, but the outbreak of the Spanish civil war at the same time resulted in their cancellation, to be resumed in Antwerp in 1937. Ultimately, no nation boycotted the 1936 Olympics.

In the 1920s and 1930s, when the Workers' Olympics were first organized, a key woman in Spanish sport circles was Ana María Sagi, a young all-round athlete who was the country's javelin champion, and also a labour organizer and director of FC Barcelona. Details of her life were suppressed during the Fascist dictatorship of 1939 to 1975, but in 2000 a biography by a Spanish author documented her career as athlete, founder of the Club Femení i d'Esports, journalist and composer of poetry that she dedicated to her former lesbian lover.[17] Sagi's writings provide some insights into the status of Spanish women in the early 1930s, as well as her own political stance. For example, she referred to herself and the other women in the Club Femení as "femenines i feministes" (feminine *and* feminist). Pointing out that Sagi rejected cycling, soccer, rugby and boxing as "unfeminine" activities that exposed women to ridicule and

DOI: 10.1057/9781137291158

harmed their cause, historian Louise Johnson summarized the Spanish feminist's politics as follows:

> just as there is a "right" way of being a feminist for many of these female journalists, which is usually defined in contrast to the Suffragettes, so there is a "right" way of being a female "esportista". Both models seek accommodation rather than confrontation (in spite of Sagi's feistiness), and central to this is the negotiation of femininity.[18]

This would suggest that in Spain, as in many other countries, questions of identity construction, in the context of liberal versus radical political strategies, occupied much of sport feminists' time and energy, not necessarily because feminists themselves chose to address these questions but because of the power of public and media opinion. Despite her leftist politics and lesbian identity, Sagi was clearly concerned about the public performance of hegemonic femininity. These apparent contradictions foreshadowed many of the later debates in sport feminist circles, beginning in the 1960s and continuing today.

In a 1984 article documenting post-war trends in workers' sports, James Riordan identified a new emphasis on "sport for all" replacing the earlier challenge to bourgeois sport. He identified "the process of decolonialisation and increasing democratization of both the Olympic movement and bourgeois sports generally (with few sports and clubs being limited to middle-class white males)" as changes that made the earlier separatist philosophy less relevant.[19] In view of *neo*colonialist trends since that time, Riordan's claim may have been over-optimistic. Moreover, since 1946, the Confédération Sportive Internationale Travailliste et Amateur (CSIT, or International Workers and Amateurs in Sports Confederation), successor to the earlier Workers' Sport Movement, has continued to organize regular International Workers' Sport Festivals attracting thousands of participants and spectators. However, Riordan was correct in predicting a change in philosophy: like the MCU, the CSIT sought IOC recognition, which was granted in 1986.[20]

Democratization of the Olympics?

In his history of the Olympics, first published in 1992, sport historian Allen Guttmann claimed that "the inclusion of women [in the 1912 Games] was one sign of gradual democratization." He went on to claim that the

DOI: 10.1057/9781137291158

"irrelevance of skin color was emphasized by the racial composition of the American team," comprising an African American, a Hawaiian and two "American Indians."[21] His 1992 statement bore a curious resemblance to a 1912 *Literary Digest* description of the American Olympic team. Commenting on the country's successes at these Olympics, the magazine article stated that, as well as "a vast population recruited from the best 'red blood'" of European nations, the team included "Indians, Hawaiians, and one Anglo-Russian."[22]

Significantly, one of the "American Indians," Jim Thorpe, was among the small number of American athletes to be stripped of his medals under the amateurism rule. Thorpe's "race" was cited by some as the cause of his alleged violation of the rule. His coach, for example, blamed Thorpe's school background for the misunderstanding: "the boys at the Indian school were children mentally and did not understand the fine distinction between amateurism and professionalism," he claimed.[23] Some accounts pointed to Avery Brundage, at that time Thorpe's teammate, as the originator of the complaint.[24]

Thorpe went on to play football and baseball professionally, and a 1950 Associated Press poll named him "greatest male athlete" of the half-century. Despite years of requests, the IOC refused to restore his medals until 1982, 29 years after his death. From 1931 to 1950, he had small roles in more than 60 Hollywood films, mostly as an "Indian" in westerns; in a few he played himself. Ironically, Thorpe himself was portrayed by a non-Native actor, Burt Lancaster, in a 1951 biographical film – not the first time that Lancaster had played an "Indian." Hollywood audiences, it seemed, were more comfortable with a white man "acting down" than with a Native man "acting up."

Returning to Guttmann's claim of "gradual democratization," I would argue that it was not only premature but also reflected an inflated view of the significance of Olympic sport for women and for oppressed minorities, as well as a failure to consider the complex factors underlying a nation's decision to include or exclude certain groups of athletes. The historical record shows that there was no straightforward correlation between the status of women, Indigenous peoples or ethnic minorities in their home countries and their representation at the Olympics. And, as historian Colin Tatz has demonstrated, the question of inclusion is as important as that of exclusion, since politicians and sport leaders used Indigenous athletes as "a special black breed of gladiators and entertainers" more than half a century before they were granted full rights as Australian citizens.[25]

DOI: 10.1057/9781137291158

"They love everything about Indigenous peoples, except the people"

The inclusion of Indigenous athletes from various "primitive" cultures at the 1904 St Louis Olympics represents one of the earliest examples of "scientific racism" applied to sport, a pattern that continues today. The so-called Anthropology Days, held in conjunction with the Olympics, were intended to prove an association between "race" and athletic ability, but at the end of this dehumanizing project, organizers concluded that these men were "inferior athletes," after all. The events "featured, in effect, a human 'zoo' with over two thousand occupants from a variety of cultures, including Ainus from Japan, Tehuelche Indians from Patagonia ... Pygmies from central Africa, a variety of Filipino groups, and representatives from more than a dozen North American Indian tribes."[26]

The cultures as well as the bodies of American, Canadian and Australian Indigenous women, men and children have long been exploited to serve the Olympic industry, frequently reduced to stereotypical roles in the cultural components of the Games. In the 1936 Berlin Olympics, this kind of cultural appropriation was at work when the Canadian Olympic Committee sent a group of dancers to perform a dance that represented an Indian legend, choreographed by a Russian, whose goal was to create "an Indian atmosphere." In a similar move almost 60 years later, the head of the Sydney 2000 bid committee sent back a preliminary design for the logo because he wanted "a bit of Aboriginality" added. Boomerangs and markings suggestive of Aboriginal dot paintings were constant features of later promotional materials.[27]

Sociologist Christine O'Bonsawin described the 1936 Indian-themed dances: "The dance group consisted of primarily female non-Native dancers clad in designs inspired by pan-Indian cliches ... performed to ... predominantly non-Native melodies." Typical of the "Indian atmosphere" approach, the Natives were depicted as "people frozen in a timeless past."[28] This portrayal of the "primitive Indian" conveniently ignored their more recent history of colonization at the hands of white settlers, the abuse they suffered in residential schools and the ongoing impacts of racism and poverty.

With the increased competition among Olympic bid cities since the 1980s, Indigenous peoples and cultures have been co-opted to boost bid committees' public relations efforts, ranging from token Indigenous representatives on bid committees to the appropriation of Native symbols

DOI: 10.1057/9781137291158

in logos and promotional materials.[29] Writing about cultural appropriation in 2003, when Vancouver was awarded the 2010 Olympics, Native activist Gord Hill aptly summarized longstanding Olympic industry attitudes: "They Love Everything about Indigenous Peoples, Except the People."[30] There were countless examples of co-optation from the early days of the Vancouver bid committee in 1998 until the Olympic closing ceremony in 2010, and beyond. In addition to the predictable "singin' and dancin'" roles assigned to Indigenous people, one of the most egregious actions was the "geographically inappropriate and culturally offensive" appropriation of the inukshuk (stacked stones) in the logo and the closing ceremony. This Inuit symbol was removed from its authentic Arctic context to serve the Olympic industry's advertising campaign, giving it the prerequisite "bit of Aboriginality." As Squamish hereditary chief Gerald Johnston explained, "It is akin to Russians planting their flag on the Parliament Buildings or the White House without permission."[31]

Taking a different approach to co-optation, and lacking an Indigenous population, the organizers of Athens' opening ceremony included a segment in which a Romani street vendor was selling watermelons from his red pickup truck, with smiling Romani women in traditional costume dancing alongside. This cheerful, colourful scene masked the cynical appropriation of a stigmatized group's culture – this after Romani families had been forcibly removed from their homes near Athens to make way for an Olympic parking lot.[32]

Until at least the 1960s, systemic racism against Indigenous peoples and racial/ethnic minorities continued unabated in the US, Canada, Australia and other western countries, as did discrimination against women in many areas, including legal status, education, employment and sport. To the extent that a "gradual democratization" of the Olympic Games occurred throughout the 20th century, it cannot be measured simply by counting the number of women and minority athletes. This belief in the redemptive and symbolic importance of Olympic sport continues to prompt many of the well-intentioned liberal western efforts to bring minority sportswomen into the Olympic fold – for example, the campaign to include more women from Muslim countries.

Ongoing themes: the first 40 years, the past 70 years

On the issues of gender inclusion and exclusion at the Olympics, most sport historians follow a predictable format that begins with the Ancient

DOI: 10.1057/9781137291158

Games in Greece, their exclusion of female athletes and female spectators, and the women-only games of Heraia, which offered three short running events. These accounts then move on to the 1890s with Coubertin's so-called revival of the ancient Games, and his explicit goal for the modern Olympics – the "exaltation of male athleticism".[33] It is important to acknowledge, however, that noted sport historians have debunked the myth of continuity between the ancient and modern Games. Rather, they have identified Coubertin's skills as a social marketer[34] and public relations expert whose success relied in large part on "dressing his games in the image of antiquity" at a time in European history when ancient Greek culture was fashionable.[35] For Coubertin, invoking the past was a useful way of justifying the present: the inclusion of ancient sports such as discus throwing[36] and the exclusion of women.

Coubertin's elaboration of "the Olympic idea" bears repeating: "the concept of a strong muscular culture based, on the one hand, on the chivalrous spirit, ... 'fair play', and on the other hand, on the aesthetic idea, the cult of beauty and grace."[37] In view of his well-known admiration of the British achievement sport model, his lesser regard for the European fitness-oriented model exemplified by gymnastics and his lifelong opposition to women's participation, it is not surprising that the early Olympic programme largely failed to integrate aesthetic appeal as well as muscular culture. Conveniently, his reference to "beauty and grace" invoked ancient Greek culture, but its expression was generally limited to the cultural programme and the opening and closing ceremonies. However, regarding contradictions in Coubertin's philosophy, former Olympic athlete, essayist and International Olympic Academy manager Nadezhda Lekarska, writing in 1973, offered this explanation: "Inconsistency not being typical of Coubertin, this deviation from his original view on the Program does not impair his personal integrity."[38] For those who followed Coubertin's every utterance, this was no doubt reassuring.

"Beauty and grace" became important themes in relation to Olympic sportswomen, generally dredged up to support conservative rationales for carefully monitored female participation in sports that did not challenge hegemonic femininity. In her so-called sociological justification, Lekarska made frequent references to the athletes who were "beautiful" and "charming" symbols of "womanly grace." She also reassured readers concerning girls' and women's alleged "fear of muscle-boundness" as a result of training, citing experts who guaranteed no muscular

DOI: 10.1057/9781137291158

"malformations."[39] And, foreshadowing the later popularity of the social control argument, Lekarska claimed that sport for girls served as a "preventive measure against social ills" such as prostitution and the use of alcohol and narcotics, vices that made it "far harder for girls to fulfil their maternal obligations."[40] A Nike advertising campaign 20 years later exploited similar myths, making the claims that, for girls and women, playing sports helped to prevent unwanted pregnancies, breast cancer and depression, while promoting self-confidence and self-esteem, and that a woman who played sport would "be more likely to leave a man" who beat her. As sociologist Melisse Lafrance explained, in addition to these "fraudulently immoral" and exaggerated claims, the messages promoted "the consumption of expensive sporting goods ... open only to those who make up the dominant class," or, one might add, to children and adolescents from working-class families who are seduced by the Nike product, "inspired by the image and essence of Michael Jordan."[41]

Continuing the same theme in 1978, the 50th anniversary of female participation in track and field, sport journalist Alfredo Narvaez observed that women's first appearance in these events "left its mark of beauty and grace in competitions where previously only male ruggedness could have been imagined."[42] With such views in circulation as recently as the 1970s, there was little room for the female athletes who lacked beauty and grace but had an abundance of the traits that made them good at achievement sport: muscular strength and endurance. A 2006 analysis of sport media coverage of women demonstrated that the preoccupation with beauty and grace continues.[43]

The earliest manifestations of female "beauty and grace" were the displays of Danish women's gymnastics in the Olympics from 1904 to 1920. These had a different purpose than the later demonstration sports, representing "a kind of competition between 'the systems of different [European] nations' ... especially with regard to aesthetics and precision."[44] They posed a challenge to the achievement sport model as well as providing a limited opportunity for female participation. As Danish historian Else Trangbaek noted, these female gymnasts have been left out of most historical accounts, although there was no shortage of attention paid to them at the time. The "charming gymnasts" were reported to have been the most photographed participants in British newspapers during the 1908 London Olympics, a mixed blessing in view of media and public preoccupation with their "femininity." Greek papers of the time referred to "the beautiful, well-built, noble, fair-haired girls"

DOI: 10.1057/9781137291158

whose "seemly" performances showed "grace, nobility and suppleness," while British papers reassured readers that the gymnasts were "under medium stature," with physiques that had "nothing of the Amazonian."[45] What was unstated in these accounts was the implication that larger, more muscular, and hence "unfeminine" women lacking such desirable and decorative features had no place on the Olympic playing field.

Trangbaek claimed that the combination of the gymnasts' expressions of "proper" womanhood and their more challenging public bodily performances constituted an important step towards greater acceptance of sportswomen. This claim needs to be qualified: the women were performing gender and ethnicity as well as gymnastics, thereby furthering the acceptance of a specific female sporting identity that did not stray far from prevailing western concepts of hegemonic femininity. To use some current examples, consider what the public and media response might have been if the gymnasts had resembled Venus Williams rather than Olga Korbut, or Martina Navratilova rather than Marylou Retton.

Women's challenges to Olympic hegemony

From the outset, a few sport leaders, male as well as female, challenged Coubertin's rigid views on women, and, from 1900, the Olympic programme began to include some events for female athletes. These were limited to sports considered compatible with current ideals of white, middle- and upper-class womanhood. Golf, tennis, archery, swimming, figure skating and fencing were the only sports for women in the six Olympics from 1900 to 1924. Photographs from the era show sportswomen wearing long-sleeved, neck-to-ankle dresses that would have allayed fears of impropriety, and, in the absence of track and field events, which were expressly forbidden by the IOC until 1928, it was unlikely that women's early participation would pose a serious threat to hegemonic femininity.

Modest swimming attire, however, presented a challenge to sport leaders, since some female swimmers were abandoning the heavy bathing dresses and stockings of the late 1800s in favour of briefer, more form-fitting swimsuits. Victorian notions of propriety prevailed even in Australia, where beach swimming during daylight hours was prohibited until the turn of the century. Some women-only hours were offered at pools on weekdays, but this restricted access for working women.[46] The

DOI: 10.1057/9781137291158

New South Wales Ladies' Amateur Swimming Association (NSWLASA) addressed the dress code problem by prohibiting its members from swimming in front of male spectators. "[It] would be alright if the men would behave themselves properly, but a lot of bad men are attracted who would make all sorts of nasty remarks and who would rather go for the spectacle than the skill," as NSWLASA president, feminist Rose Scott, explained.[47] She predicted, too, that the mingling of the sexes would result in "too much boldness and rudeness"[48] and warned that male voyeurism could lead to society's return "to the primitive state of the blacks,"[49] a racist comment that reflected the white majority's views of Aboriginal peoples at the time, and for many decades to come.

Presumably Scott and her colleagues believed that it was easier to change the rules of the women's association than to attempt to change men's behaviour, thereby following a strategy similar to that of their American counterparts in the Women's Division of the National Amateur Athletic Association. Prompted by concerns over improper behaviour on the part of male spectators, coaches, trainers, masseurs and journalists, they called for female-only coaching and training staff, an end to inter-school and intercollegiate competition and, unsurprisingly, a ban on female athletes in the Olympics. Theirs was not a "separate-but-equal" approach, but rather a "separate-and-different" strategy aimed at maximizing female physical recreation – closer to the fitness and body experience models than the achievement model – while avoiding the excessive commercialization, competitiveness and elitism that characterized male sport.[50] There was a clear element of protectiveness, too, which some historians view as patronizing. Certainly there was no scientific basis for treating females like fragile flowers, and the Women's Division approach held back talented sportswomen. On the other hand, the threat of exploitation of young female athletes was real, as was the potential for harassment and abuse.

Citing propriety concerns, Scott unsuccessfully opposed Australian women's participation in the 1912 swimming events in Stockholm, the first time that women's swimming was included in the Olympic programme. Equally important (and infrequently documented), she objected to the Olympics on pacifist grounds, no doubt aware of the non-pacifist nature of the men's programme, and its emphasis on guns and aggression.[51] At the time of the 1912 Stockholm Olympics, there were 17 shooting events (including shooting live pigeons and running deer) as well as wrestling, judo and fencing. (Boxing, introduced in 1900, was absent from the 1912 programme because it was prohibited in Sweden.[52])

DOI: 10.1057/9781137291158

On the subject of women-only swimming competition, Australian historian Veronica Raszeja explained that "By excluding men from women's races, the NSWLASA allowed the women to retain their aquatic freedom, and their competitive edge. The alternatives of no competition ... or the adoption of cumbersome skirted costumes were thus astutely avoided."[53] In other words, a seemingly conservative position on the part of these early feminist sport leaders succeeded as a strategy that gave Australian women a "separate-but-equal" context in which to develop swimming skills. Although the men of the Australian Olympic Committee withheld financial assistance, supportive individuals and groups organized fund-raising to cover the travel expenses of the country's two top female swimmers, Fanny Durack and Mina Wylie, together with the mandatory chaperone, to participate in the 1912 Games in Stockholm. In contrast, when the male leaders of the American Olympic Committee and Amateur Athletic Union who controlled American women's sport decided that no women would be allowed to swim in the 1912 Olympics, there was no outpouring of public support or funding for their participation.

Australia had achieved swimming success in 1900 with its sole swimmer, Frederick Lane, winning two gold medals, and the inclusion of women's events in 1912 provided another important opportunity for international recognition, particularly in light of Durack's established international reputation. The Americans, on the other hand, were not relying on women to bring home medals: they had ranked first in overall medals in 1896 and 1904, and second in 1900 and 1908, based almost entirely upon male athletes' performances.

At the time of the 1912 Olympics, Durack and Wylie were already well known for their swimming achievements. As a child, Durack had trained during the limited "ladies' hours" at a Sydney pool, while Wylie had the advantage of coming from a swimming family: her father operated Wylie's Baths near Coogee Beach from 1907 on. Adjacent to these baths was a women-only pool (which still operates as a women's and children's pool) where Durack and Wylie were reported to have practised, although at 20 metres long and about 1 metre deep, it did not provide optimal conditions for training for 100 and 220 metre races. Despite these obstacles, both women's swimming times qualified them for the Olympics, with Durack holding three world records by 1912. Among the 27 women in the 100 metre freestyle event, the two Australians took first and second places. In short, although their stories are a key part of the

DOI: 10.1057/9781137291158

Australian sport narrative, Durack and Wylie were not products of a fully democratized society. Rather, they were two women with unusual talent and commitment, and a combination of circumstances worked in their favour, bringing them, and a young nation, international recognition.

In 1914, the American ban on women's Olympic participation was successfully challenged by Charlotte Epstein, founder of the National Women's Life Saving League in 1914 and co-founder of the New York Women's Swimming Association in 1917. Originally a court stenographer, Epstein and other working women enjoyed recreational swimming at the end of the workday. She persuaded the American Athletic Union to allow female swimmers to register for and to compete in the 1920 Antwerp Olympics, subsequently coached successful Olympic swimmers for 22 years and was manager of the US women's Olympic swim teams in 1920, 1924 and 1932. Invited to be the coach of the 1936 team, she refused the offer and resigned from the US Olympic Committee in protest against American participation in the Nazi Olympics. In 1935, she was involved in selecting teams for the second Maccabiah Games.[54]

There are countless stories of other countries' "first women" that sport historians appropriately document. After all, with few team sports for men and none for women before the 1960s, public and media attention focused on individual athletes, not teams, and sport historiography reflects this. However, generalizations about a country's social and political conditions based on the Olympic performances of individual women or members of racial/ethnic minorities are problematic. In the 1924 Paris Olympics, for example, the British team of 232 athletes included 31 women, yet British women did not have full voting rights until 1928, and the deeply entrenched class system was showing few signs of changing, thereby doubly disadvantaging working-class women. Clearly, 31 individual "successes" tell us very little about a "successful" society. Yet the practice of treating Olympic participation as a symbol of a country's progress continues today, and this myth recently found its fullest expression in the rhetoric about the Beijing 2008 Olympics and China's purported steps towards ending human rights violations.[55]

The Women's Olympics

The short but significant history of the Women's Olympics, organized by the Fédération Sportive Féminine Internationale (FSFI) in 1921 under the leadership of Alice Milliat of France and Sophie Eliott Lynn of Great

DOI: 10.1057/9781137291158

Britain, has generally been interpreted as a strategy, or even a bluff, to pressure the International Amateur Athletic Federation (IAAF) and the IOC to take female athletes seriously and, more specifically, to force them to expand the Olympic track and field programme to include women's events.[56]

An alternative explanation is that the FSFI, somewhat like the Australian women's swimming federation and other women-only initiatives of the time, sought to establish autonomous women-only sporting competition. American and British women were involved in the FSFI, and their political positions were probably shaped by the ongoing suffrage movements in their respective countries, where women were not only seeking the right to vote, but also rejecting the notion of taking subservient positions in men's organizations. French historians recently examined the complexity of Milliat's goals, concluding that, although she wanted the full range of competitive sports open to women, at the same time she was determined to keep control of the FSFI in women's hands.[57] Ahead of her time, she understood and tried to prevent the negative consequences of a liberal/reform approach to women's rights in sport.

In terms of promoting international sporting competition for women, the FSFI was, in fact, more successful than both the IAAF and the IOC in the 1920s and 1930s. Originally comprising delegates from only five countries – England, the United States, France, Italy and Czechoslovakia – the FSFI organized four Women's Olympics (1922, 1926, 1930 and 1934), attracting hundreds of athletes and thousands of spectators. There were 15,000 spectators present at the Paris Games in 1924, and it may not have helped the women's cause when a French newspaper compared Milliat's success to Coubertin's.[58] By the 1930s, female athletes from 19 countries were offered 15 events: high jump, shot put, javelin and 12 running events, the longest at 800 metres.

On the Olympic front, the FSFI's lobbying efforts resulted in the inclusion of 5 track and field events in the 1928 women's Olympic programme – 10 fewer than in the FSFI games. By 1926, the IAAF had assumed complete control of women's track and field, having decreed that there could not be separate men's and women's athletics federations.[59] Also in 1926, the IOC compelled the FSFI to stop using the brand name "Olympic" (although one official record stated that it had merely "pressed for the withdrawal of the term Olympic ... ").[60] Eight years later, however, Milliat's statement to the IOC demonstrated that, for her, the struggle was not over. In 1934, she wrote:

DOI: 10.1057/9781137291158

The FSFI will accept to give up the Women's World Games if a full programme of women's athletics is included in the Olympic Games and under the condition that women are represented within the IOC. The FSFI also notes that the IOC is less and less willing to open the Olympic Games to women in all sports. For now, it is preferable to keep the Women's World Games which accept all female sports.[61]

In May 1935, the IOC discussed a letter from Milliat proposing that it exclude all female participation in the Olympic Games, on the grounds that the FSFI was organizing its own quadrennial games.[62] A year later, several French sport federations had integrated women's organizations, and the French government had stopped funding the FSFI, which was subsequently disbanded.

A well-documented aspect of the FSFI's hollow victory vis-à-vis the IAAF and the IOC was the elimination of the 800 metre race from the Olympic women's programme following the 1928 Games, ostensibly on medical grounds; it was not reinstated until 1960. Various male authorities claimed that a race of this length was too strenuous for women, merely because some women lay down on the track after the race. Since women had already run this distance in two earlier FSFI games, and since media distortions and fabrication of the facts (false claims that *most* competitors dropped out and collapsed) were uncovered shortly after,[63] the IOC may have been less worried about women's health or propriety than about the public image of the Games. Tired, sweating women were not exactly a selling point in 1928, and little has changed in more than 80 years.

By 1932, a grand total of 21 female athletes were competing in the Olympic Games, many from countries where women's rights were gradually receiving wider recognition and where women's sport leaders were gaining influence: Europe, Great Britain, the US, Canada and Australia, for example. In 1926, British IOC member Harry Barclay had told the IAAF that British sportswomen would not be governed by men, and that the British association did not want to control women's track and field, but his advocacy efforts had failed to stop the IAAF takeover. In an unusual display of solidarity with women, Britain refused to send a female track and field team to the 1928 Amsterdam Olympics.[64] Similarly, in 1929, after the IOC voted to eliminate all women's track and field events, the president of the American Athletic Union and IAAF member Gustavus Kirby recommended that the IAAF withdraw all *male* athletes from the 1932 Los Angeles Olympics unless women could compete.

DOI: 10.1057/9781137291158

Faced with that threat, the IOC reversed its 1929 decision in 1931, and women's track and field remained on the programme.[65]

Inclusions and exclusions

Although the 20th century was well under way before many European countries, as well as Canada, the US and Great Britain, had granted women full rights as citizens, sportswomen from these countries competed in many of the early Olympics. It is possible to attribute these patterns to tokenism – a few female athletes serving as unofficial ambassadors to enhance their countries' reputations in the international community – but there were other structural factors at work that influenced female participation.

No Asian country sent a female athlete until 1928, when Japanese all-round track athlete Kinue Hitomi won a silver medal in the high-profile 800 metre race. Her international successes, including a record-breaking long jump at the 1926 Women's World Games, were attributed in part to her "unusual physique" for an Asian woman: she reportedly had well-developed leg muscles and was 5 feet 7 inches tall.[66] For women from Asia or elsewhere with less "unusual" physiques – women who were shorter and lighter than Hitomi – the women's programme offered limited opportunities. Eurocentric sports – tennis, golf and archery, for example – dominated the programme, and gymnastics, a sport well suited to smaller female physiques, was not introduced until 1928.

Since elitist sport clubs offering golf, tennis and figure skating were not accessible to women who lacked time and discretionary income, the introduction of track and field events allowed for greater participation of working-class women in western countries, many of whom joined athletic clubs sponsored by local businesses or organizations such as the YWCA and YWHA. In an era of non-specialization, many sportswomen, including the members of the Canadian women's track and field team at the 1928 Amsterdam Olympics, were accomplished all-round athletes, competing in several track and field events as well as playing softball and basketball at home.

While the history of Olympic sportswomen from western countries has been relatively well documented, there were countless other women who enjoyed high levels of sporting success. Three elderly women whom I interviewed in Toronto in 1983 were contemporaries of the 1928

DOI: 10.1057/9781137291158

Canadian women's team. As well as track and field, they competed in softball leagues in summer and basketball in winter. One was a competitive diver, and another, competing in running broad jump, narrowly missed a place on the 1932 Olympic team. As for many sportswomen of the day, their interest began in childhood, usually with encouragement from parents and brothers.[67]

During this era, racism in the US appears to have trumped medal-winning potential, as is evident in the case of two African American athletes, Louise Stokes and Tydie Pickett. They had qualified for the 1932 Olympic track and field team; however, en route to Los Angeles, the coach decided to replace them with two white women (having already segregated them by giving them a separate room in the service area of the hotel and excluding them from the team banquet). In 1936, Stokes again qualified for the team, and people in her hometown of Walden, Massachusetts, raised money to send her to Berlin, but again at the last minute the coach replaced her with a white woman.[68] Significantly, it was at these same Olympics that the four gold medals won by African American track and field athlete Jesse Owens were widely celebrated as a blow to Hitler's view of Aryan superiority, as was the fact that African American athletes won 13 medals in track and field. Significantly, 10 of the 67 male athletes on the American track and field team were Black, but there were only 2 Black women among the 16 female athletes. Overall, of the 109 athletes on the American team, 17 were Black, and these athletes participated in only 4 out of 26 sports.[69] These patterns of inclusion and exclusion reflect the combined impacts of discrimination based on gender, class and race in sport contexts.

The "new woman"

American all-round athlete and champion golfer Mildred "Babe" Didrikson was a member of the 1932 track and field team from which Stokes and Pickett had been excluded. Her record-breaking performances resulted in three medals, but the Amateur Athletic Union subsequently suspended her amateur status after her name was used to advertise a car. They then offered to reinstate her, but she had decided to play golf as a professional, winning 82 tournaments during her career. She continued to play and excel at baseball, basketball and several other sports, sometimes joining men's teams.[70]

DOI: 10.1057/9781137291158

Several aspects of Didrikson's identity are significant, including her immigrant and working-class roots and her "cockiness," as lesbian author Patricia Warren called it. Her "tomboyish" appearance and short haircut prompted sportswriters to call her an "Amazon" – a code word for a lesbian athlete. Whether she was lesbian or bisexual is not the most important question. Rather, as Warren explained, the non-conforming image that regularly appeared on newsreels across the country gave a generation of girls a validating alternative to the "perfect American feminine" girl – Didrikson was a "tomboy" and an athlete.[71] She played herself (a "sports star") in one of the rare films of the 1950s on women in sport, the Katharine Hepburn and Spencer Tracy movie *Pat and Mike*. Hepburn's character was a champion golfer and tennis player (and Hepburn herself was accomplished in these sports). The film featured some other athletes playing themselves: Gussie Moran and Alice Marble (tennis) and Beverly Hanson and Helen Dettweiler (golf).

Unsurprisingly, homophobic press coverage of Didrikson was common, even after she married and tried to develop a more "feminine" image through dress, makeup and hairstyle. These efforts, together with her much-reported statement "I know I'm not pretty, but I try to be graceful," are poignant reminders of the hostility she experienced.[72]

Similar themes surfaced almost 80 years later in relation to the controversy surrounding South African sprinter Caster Semenya's sex/gender when a "glamorous" photo appeared on a 2009 magazine cover following her beauty "makeover."[73] And yet, from a different perspective, that same cover photo revealed the core of the controversy, that is, the superficiality of *image*. Did Semenya simply need a new hairstyle, some makeup and a fashionable black dress to appear more "feminine" and satisfy the critics?

Whether Didrikson's marriage-and-makeover response was pragmatic or a personal reaction to public criticism is difficult to determine. Unlike most of her female contemporaries, she could draw on an impressive record of sporting achievements as a source of self-esteem that went well beyond reliance on her appearance and lifestyle. Despite their hostility, it was impossible for the media to ignore her sport performance, and among the many accolades she received were five Woman Athlete of the Year awards from Associated Press and, in 1950, Woman Athlete of the Half Century.

The same year, Canadian sportswriters named another all-round athlete, Fanny "Bobbie" Rosenfeld, Female Athlete of the Half Century.

DOI: 10.1057/9781137291158

A stenographer in a Toronto factory during the 1920s and 1930s, she was a champion track and field athlete and tennis player, and a key member of the Canadian track and field team at the 1928 Olympics, winning gold and silver medals. One of Rosenfeld's teammates, Ethel Catherwood, became the media's favourite athlete. Dubbed the "Saskatoon Lily" by the press, she became the most photographed woman at the Games. Rosenfeld, although a superior all-round athlete, lacked the prerequisite "beauty and grace." Of course, it was somewhat easier to maintain one's grace and beauty as a high jumper than as a competitor in the 100 and 800 metre races as well as a member of the 400 metre relay team.

Nearly 50 years later, in their book *Olympic Gold*, Canadian sport historians Frank Cosentino and Glynn Leyshon referred to Catherwood's "statuesque beauty and icy poise," and devoted a full chapter to her. Apparently Rosenthal's extensive achievements did not merit their own chapter; they were incorporated into the chapter on the 400 metre women's relay team, and one of those runners, Myrtle Cook, appeared on the cover of the book.[74]

Another competitor, alongside Didrikson, in the 1932 track events was Australian Eileen Wearne. She did not place in her events, but the Australian officials' report defended her on the grounds that "The masculine type of girl [Didrikson] has an advantage over the feminine type – a class that Miss Wearne represents. A perfect little lady and a credit to the team."[75] This kind of subjective and inappropriate commentary might be expected in newspaper or magazine coverage, but its appearance in an official report gives some indication of the systemic barriers facing non-conforming female athletes.

Didrikson's and Rosenfeld's identities and careers were parallel in many ways: so-called tomboys from working-class immigrant families, excellent all-round athletes, internationally successful in track and field, and with short hair. The nickname "Bobbie" referred to Rosenfeld's bobbed haircut, at a time when longer hair was the fashion for white, middle-class women. The salience of sportswomen's hairstyles was yet another indicator of public and media preoccupation with their appearance rather than their performance. As late as 1973, the obsession with hair was evident in an Australian media account that praised sprinter Raelene Boyle because "unlike the women athletes who chop their hair short for speed, Raelene kept her hair long."[76] And from the 1980s on, there appears to have been an unwritten rule (or perhaps an actual

DOI: 10.1057/9781137291158

policy) that women playing team sports at the national or international levels must have ponytails.

Rosenfeld, however, did not follow Didrikson's path by having a "femininity makeover." Nor did she get married, a perceived omission that did not pass unnoticed, then or now. As recently as 1999, a sport history article on Rosenfeld's life referred to "*allegations* of her lesbianism" (emphasis added), and included the following item in a timeline of her "most salient athletic achievements": "1969: She passed away on November 13, at age 66, childless and having never married."[77]

In contrast to these authors' heteronormative tone (and the irrelevance of Rosenfeld's marital and motherhood status), a more perceptive and validating observation came from journalist Robert Fulford, a *Globe and Mail* colleague of Rosenfeld in the 1930s and 1940s, when she was working as a sports journalist:

> Bobbie was the first lesbian I knew as such, and every day her moment of greatest happiness – happiness I could see her almost physically trying to hide, for reasons it took me years to understand – coincided with her companion's arrival at her office to pick her up after work.[78]

There is no doubt, however, that there was a price to pay for sportswomen who were seen as sexually non-conforming, even in the early decades of the century before more overt, explicitly homophobic responses were common.

The reproductive status of sportswomen has long attracted medical, public and media attention. Dutch track and field athlete Fanny Blankers-Koen, who participated in the 1936 Berlin Olympics, also took part in the 1948 Games, when she was 30 years of age and mother of two children. According to one account, perhaps embellished to counter accusations that she was a "bad mother," Blankers-Koen "wheeled the baby carriage to the Amsterdam stadium and parked it near the track, so she could watch her baby while she ran."[79] Ever mindful of the need to establish the heterosexual credentials of female athletes, the media dubbed her "The Flying Dutch Housewife," and the housewife association has been an ongoing theme since the 1950s. As Australian historian Marian Stell pointed out, hurdler Shirley Strickland, who had won Olympic medals and had written a thesis on cosmic particle detection, was still described as a housewife in accounts of her winning performance at the 1956 Melbourne Olympics.[80] The trend persisted into the 1970s and 1980s, when Australian journalists quizzed female athletes

DOI: 10.1057/9781137291158

about juggling their duties as good wives and mothers with their athletic training programmes.

Stell's summation of attitudes during these decades applied to female athletes in most western countries: "not only did they have to be world champions, gourmet chefs, selfless housewives and supermums, they had to look like models in the process."[81] Even swimmer Dawn Fraser, notorious for her extracurricular escapades at the 1964 Tokyo Olympics and her generally non-conforming persona, got drawn into the "femininity" debate in the 1950s when she asserted that "despite the constant accent on building up strength, I don't think it's necessary at any stage for a girl athlete to lose her femininity."[82]

Heroes, but no heroines?

Numerous histories of the Olympics have documented the links between sportsmen and nationhood,[83] and the ways in which national identity and international status were associated with medal rankings – this despite the longstanding directive in the Olympic Charter that "The IOC and the OCOG [Organizing Committee for the Olympic Games] shall not draw up any global ranking per country."[84] Women, regardless of their sporting successes, seem to have lacked the prerequisites for national icon status, at least in the early decades of the Olympics. This was not necessarily a disadvantage.

In her discussion of "manly displays" at the early Games, historian Lia Paradis focused on the attention paid to individual men, most notably the winners of the marathon. This event was not part of the ancient Games, but, as Paradis explained, "the myth of the self-sacrificing messenger was too good a story and provided exactly the spectacle that the new games needed."[85] Even though he collapsed and was helped across the finish line, and then disqualified, Italian Dorando Pietri became the hero of the 1908 London Olympics because he followed the rules of competition and persevered to the end. In an era marked by international tensions, "the Olympics suggested that men could compete honorably even if their nations could not."[86]

Male medal-winners gained iconic status as early as the 1920s and 1930s – Finnish runner Paavo Nurmi and American swimmer Johnny Weissmuller, for example. This trend reflected the growing political and economic importance of sport at the national and international levels,

DOI: 10.1057/9781137291158

facilitated by the improved communication of sport news through print media, radio, newsreels and films. In contrast, the limited number of women's events in the Olympic programme resulted in a very small pool of potential national icons. Many of these women received enthusiastic welcomes, as well as gifts, cash and an occasional Hollywood film offer, when they returned home, but their fame was short-lived.

Two notable exceptions were Sonja Henie and Esther Williams, both heterosexually attractive, white women whose appearance and sporting performances were compatible with prevailing norms of femininity. A champion Norwegian figure skater, Henie was recruited by 20th Century Fox in 1936 following her Olympic victories at the 1932 and 1936 Games, and acted in 11 films, ranking as Hollywood's third most successful actor after Shirley Temple and Clark Gable.[87] Similarly, champion swimmer Esther Williams performed in several films in the 1940s and 1950s, pioneering a style of water ballet that later became synchronized swimming.[88] Looking at her filmed performances through 21st-century eyes, one is struck by the simplicity and absence of artifice, in contrast to more recent trends such as adolescent female gymnasts' flirtatious floor routines.

Politicizing athletes

There is extensive documentation of Fascist and Nazi states' uses and abuses of sport as a political tool since the 1920s, with the 1936 Berlin Olympics representing the most salient example.[89] Totalitarian regimes in Russia, Italy and Germany used sport and athletic bodies to symbolize the strength and unity of the new social order. While the male body, emblematic of both athletic and military superiority, was best suited for these purposes, female athletes had their uses. In Fascist Italy in the 1930s, Italian track and field athlete Trebisonda Valla was reconfigured as the "glittering icon of Fascist femininity."[90] In the early Fascist years, both Mussolini and the Pope had opposed women's participation in sport, and in 1932 the Pope had prohibited the Italian women's team from participating in the Los Angeles Olympics. (He had also condemned women's track and field events in 1928, but the majority of IOC members voted in favour of their inclusion.)

Valla's spectacular successes soon attracted the attention of the Fascist authorities, who saw a role for her as the symbol of new Fascist womanhood – the "Superwoman" who would complement the "Superman." But,

DOI: 10.1057/9781137291158

as historian Gigliola Gori pointed out, the subservient status of "ordinary" Fascist women remained unchanged. Gori's statement implied, unintentionally, that more widespread social change might be expected following the public recognition of one individual sportswoman. A more realistic assessment would point to tokenism on the part of political and religious authorities whose agendas were served by valorizing exceptional women, a recurring theme in the history of Olympic sport.

During this era, according to Guttmann, liberal-democratic countries were "relatively indifferent" to their athletes' international successes or failure.[91] However, American historian Mark Dyreson has convincingly countered this claim of "indifference." In his analysis of Johnny Weissmuller's role in the "federal blueprint for selling American culture to the world," he demonstrated how the US government used achievement sport to promote American commerce and culture. After Weissmuller's Olympic swimming successes in 1924 and 1928 led to a Hollywood career as Tarzan, "[his] face and body would be projected around the world as an advertisement for American lifestyles."[92] The Tarzan phenomenon pioneered the trend of using a male sporting celebrity to deliver a global consumer market for American sport and leisure goods (and eventually for products ranging from margarine to Mercedes). At the same time, Weissmuller's image exported the idea of a specific type of American muscular masculinity to the rest of the world. His usefulness on these fronts appears to have overcome any disadvantage that his Jewish background might have presented, despite the anti-Semitism of the era. Olympic athletes who later played the Tarzan role included another swimmer, Larry "Buster" Crabbe, a gymnast, a shot-putter, a decathlete and a pole vaulter – all white men.

Another American Olympic swimming champion (1912, 1920 and 1924) who subsequently had an acting career was Duke Kahanamoku. He was routinely referred to as "the Hawaiian" (as recently as 1995 in an *Olympic Review* article), even though Hawaii was annexed by the US in 1898, making Kahanamoku a member of the *American* team.[93] When it suited American nationalist interests to promote America's "multiracial superiority" in sport, however, the inclusion of North American Indians, Hawaiians and other minorities was held up as evidence of the success of the melting-pot model.[94]

The victories of African American Jesse Owens in the 1936 Berlin Olympics only generated fleeting iconic status for him, although Coca-Cola recognized his potential as a marketing tool. He made a triumphant

DOI: 10.1057/9781137291158

return to the US, with the other members of the American team, in New York, where Mayor La Guardia praised him as "an American *boy*" (emphasis added), as well as a hero's welcome in his hometown of Cleveland.[95] He later became an outspoken critic of racism in the US, and was shunned by the American Olympic Committee and by Avery Brundage, IOC president from 1952 to 1972.

Black power

One of the earliest examples of protest initiated by Olympic athletes was the planned African American boycott of the 1968 Mexico City Games, which the Olympic Project for Human Rights (OPHR) began to organize in 1966 under the leadership of Harry Edwards. This group of male athletes was protesting the racism faced by Black people in the US and expressing solidarity with Blacks in South Africa under Apartheid. In addition, they called for the restoration of Muhammad Ali's boxing title, which had been stripped from him because of his anti-Vietnam War stance. Finally, they demanded that Brundage, infamous for his long-standing anti-Semitic and white supremacist views, be removed from office. Although the boycott did not take place, the Black Power protest on the podium by African American runners John Carlos and Tommie Smith,[96] supported by Australian Peter Norman, has rightly gone down in history as one of the most powerful and memorable political statements ever made by Olympic athletes.[97]

As well as the obvious political significance of the 1968 Black protest, these events and the official reactions reinforced views of "good" and "bad" Black Americans. When news of the planned Mexico City boycott came out, Brundage dispatched Jesse Owens to play the part of the "good Black American" who could persuade Carlos and Smith to abandon their planned political protest.[98] By this time, Owens was promoting the Olympics as helping "bridge the gap of misunderstanding of people in this country,"[99] but he failed to dissuade Carlos and Smith, who were subsequently ejected from the Olympic Village, vilified in the American press and ostracized for years to come.

Meanwhile, African American boxing champion George Foreman had a very different experience at the 1968 Games. In a 1984 interview, describing his feelings in Mexico City as he waved a small American flag in front of a cheering crowd, he said, "I was so proud. I wasn't black or

DOI: 10.1057/9781137291158

white. I was American."[100] At the time, Black athletes saw his flag-waving as an anti-solidarity display, a view that his later statement certainly substantiated.

Carlos had no illusions about the fleeting fame associated with Olympic success. Observing how Black athletes often thought that Olympic medals would protect them from racism, he warned, "even if you won a medal, it ain't going to save your momma, it ain't going to save your sister or children. It might give you fifteen minutes of fame, but what about the rest of your life?"[101] The myths surrounding Olympic success continue to be perpetuated. Speaking at a University of Toronto panel discussion on Olympic athletes in 2012, sports journalist Teddy Katz told the audience about a coach whose motivational style included the following advice to a young athlete: "Friends come and go, but an Olympic medal goes on forever."[102]

In later reflections on the protests, Carlos acknowledged that OPHR had failed to open its doors to Black women, although it had welcomed the support of the white (Harvard) men of the American crew team. Despite women's exclusion, African American runner Wyomia Tyus publicly dedicated the women's relay gold medal win to Carlos and Smith.

Black men, Black women

Discussing the "overrepresentation" of Black women in high performance sport in the 1960s and 1970s, Harry Edwards suggested that there was greater acceptance of female athletes among African Americans than among white Americans. While acknowledging the limited sociological research on the topic at the time (1973), he hypothesized that the instrumental-versus-expressive gender binary was less sharply defined in Black society. The greater proportion of woman-led Black families (then estimated at one-third) resulted in greater acceptance of women in instrumental roles, including that of successful athlete, he claimed. For a white woman, athletic ability raised suspicions about her "womanliness," and she would be steered towards more expressive roles such as that of cheerleader.[103] Later feminist research on "femininity" generally confirmed his theory about the constraints on white middle-class sportswomen,[104] but many complex questions relating to Black women's participation in sport remain under-researched.

DOI: 10.1057/9781137291158

At the time that Edwards was writing, Black women had a high profile in intercollegiate sports, with predominantly Black colleges offering extensive sport programmes for women, particularly in track and field. In proportion to their numbers in the American population, Black women were overrepresented on the US Olympic track and field teams: 12 of 18 women in 1960, and 21 of 36 women in 1980.[105] However, at the time of the 1980 Moscow Olympics, there were only 4 Black women on the US basketball team, 2 in rowing, 2 in volleyball and 1 in fencing. Of the American men's teams in the same Olympics, all 11 boxers were Black, as were 10 of the 12 basketball players and 3 of the 20 wrestlers. There was no Black representation, male or female, in any other Olympic sport.

This pattern suggests that systemic factors contributed to Black women's track and field careers in the 1960s and 1970s, including the relative financial and geographic accessibility of track and field clubs (and the barriers in accessing golf, tennis, swimming and other sports clubs) and expanded intercollegiate sport programmes after the 1972 Title IX legislation. Although the civil rights movement removed many of the barriers experienced by Black athletes earlier in the century, a kind of selective racism resulted in the exclusion of some Black athletes and the elevation of others as national heroes.

One of the marks of celebrity status – a Hollywood acting career – was rarely offered to Black Olympic athletes. A 1995 tally of athletes-turned-actors in the *Olympic Review* included no Black women and only three Black or ethnic minority men: decathlete Rafer Johnson in the 1950s and boxers Mark Breland and José Torres in the 1970s and 1980s.[106] Curiously, the article added Johnson's name to the list of (white) Olympic athletes who had followed Johnny Weissmuller in the role of Tarzan since the 1930s. However, in his 1960s Tarzan films, Johnson had played "a jungle badman," not the lead role,[107] and the whiteness of the Tarzan role remained intact.

Conclusion

Discrimination based on gender, class, race and ethnicity, together with the "beauty and grace" prerequisite for female athletes, characterized Olympic sport throughout the 20th century and continues in various forms today. In the face of the Olympic industry's selective inclusions and exclusions, several marginalized groups challenged Olympic industry hegemony by

DOI: 10.1057/9781137291158

organizing alternative international sport competitions, with varying degrees of success. In the next chapter, the focus will be on sports conducted in two contested sites: the swimming pool and the skating rink.

Notes

1 Terminology has changed since the 1960s as sexual minority rights movements have evolved. Initially the term "gay" was used in western countries, then *lesbian* and *gay*, and by the 21st century, *LGBT* or *LGBTQ* (lesbian, gay, bisexual, transgendered/transsexual, queer). I will use the term that is most appropriate for each specific historical period.

2 H. Lenskyj, *Olympic Industry Resistance: Challenging Olympic Power and Propaganda* (Albany, NY: SUNY Press, 2008), Conclusion.

3 For more comprehensive coverage of independent international games, see J. Riordan, The Workers' Olympics, in A. Tomlinson and G. Whannel (eds), *Five Ring Circus: Money, Power and Politics at the Olympic Games* (London: Pluto, 1984), 98–112; A. Suchet, D. Jorand, and J. Tuppen (2010) History and Geography of a Forgotten Olympic Project: The Spring Games, *Sport in History* 30:4, 570–87.

4 R. Gechtman, Socialist Mass Politics through Sport: The Bund's Morgnshtern in Poland, 1926–1939, *Journal of Sport History* 26:2 (1999), 346–52.

5 Deutsch quoted in Gechtman, 334.

6 Ibid., 343.

7 Ibid., 333.

8 For a critical review of research on the role model concept, see Lenskyj, *Olympic Industry Resistance*, chapters 5 and 6.

9 Dr. Tim Noakes quoted on M. Ginnane (dir.), Too Fast To Be a Woman, *The Passionate Eye* (Ottawa: CBC Television, August 31, 2011).

10 Gechtman, 347.

11 G. Pfister and T. Niewerth, Gymnastics and Sport in Germany, *Journal of Sport History* 26:2 (1999), 287–325.

12 G. Eisen, Olympic Ideology & Jewish Values: Conflict or Accommodation? in R. Barney et al. (eds), *Olympic Perspectives*, Proceedings of the Third International Symposium for Olympic Research (London, ON: University of Western Ontario, 1996), 121–6.

13 G. Eisen, Jewish History and the Ideology of Modern Sport: Approaches and Interpretations, *Journal of Sport History* 25:3 (1998), 515.

14 The Maccabiah Games, International Jewish Sports Hall of Fame web site, http://www.jewishsports.net/the_maccabiah_games.htm

15 The Chairman of the "Maccabi World Union" Writes to Us, *Olympic Review* 77 (February 1962), 45.

DOI: 10.1057/9781137291158

16   D. Large, The Nazi Olympics: Berlin 1936, in H. Lenskyj and S. Wagg (eds), *Handbook of Olympic Studies* (Basingstoke, UK: Palgrave Macmillan, 2012), 48.
17   P. Warren, *The Lavender Locker Room* (Beverly Hills, CA: Wildcat Press, 2006), 151–67.
18   L. Johnson, Women Writing on Physical Culture in Pre-Civil War Catalonia, working paper (Berkeley, CA: Institute of European Studies, University of California, Berkeley, 2004), http://escholarship.org/uc/item/0bc654jh
19   Riordan, 108.
20   Confédération Sportive Internationale Travailliste et Amateur (CSIT) – International Workers and Amateurs in Sports Confederation web site, http://www.csit.tv/en
21   A. Guttmann, *The Olympics* (Champaign, IL: University of Illinois Press, 1992), 33.
22   J. Nendel, New Hawaiian Monarchy: The Media Representations of Duke Kahanamoku, 1911–1912, *Journal of Sport History* 31:1 (2004), 32–52.
23   Associated Press and Grolier Enterprises, *Pursuit of Excellence: The Olympic Story* (Danbury CT: Grolier Enterprises, 1979), 70.
24   S. Wagg, Tilting at Windmills? Olympic Politics and the Spectre of Amateurism, in Lenskyj and Wagg, 326.
25   C. Tatz, *Aborigines in Sport*, Australian Society for Sport History No. 3 (Adelaide: Flinders University, 1987).
26   D. Lunt and M. Dyreson, The 1904 Olympic Games: Triumph or Nadir? in Lenskyj and Wagg, 43–59.
27   H. Lenskyj, *The Best Olympics Ever? Social Impacts of Sydney 2000* (Albany, NY: SUNY Press, 2002), 79.
28   C. O'Bonsawin, An Indian Atmosphere, in K. Wamsley et al. (eds), *Cultural Relations Old and New: The Transitory Olympic Ethos*, Proceedings of the Seventh International Symposium for Olympic Research (London, ON: University of Western Ontario, 2004), 105–11.
29   Lenskyj, *Best Olympics Ever?*; C. O'Bonsawin, The Conundrum of Ilanaaq: First Nations Representation and the 2010 Vancouver Winter Olympics, in N. Crowther, R. Barney, and M. Heine (eds), *Cultural Imperialism in Action: Critiques in the Global Olympic Trust* (London, ON: University of Western Ontario, 2006), 387–94.
30   G. Hill, They Love Everything about Indigenous Peoples, Except the People. Vancouver Media Co-op web site (2003, posted October 27, 2009), http://vancouver.mediacoop.ca/audio/2003
31   Johnston quoted in C. O'Bonsawin, The Conundrum of Ilanaaq, 389.
32   L. Feeney and C. Hickey (dir.), *Garlic and Watermelons* (Chicago, IL: Pattern Films, 2006).
33   DeFranz, The Olympic Games: Our Birthright to Sport, in G. Cohen (ed.), *Women in Sport: Issues and Controversies* (Newbury Park, CA: Sage, 1993), 185–92.

DOI: 10.1057/9781137291158

34 D. Chatziefstathiou, Pierre de Coubertin: Man and Myth, in Lenskyj and Wagg, 26–40.

35 B. Kidd, The Myth of the Ancient Games, in Tomlinson and Whannel, 71–83.

36 M. Golden, The Ancient Games and the Modern: Mirror and Mirage, in Lenskyj and Wagg, 15–25.

37 P. de Coubertin, "We Want to Go Ever Forward": The Trustees of the Olympic Idea, *Olympic Review* (January 1987), 46–8 (originally published in *Olympic Review*, July 1908, 108–10).

38 N. Lekarska, *Essays and Studies on Olympic Problems* (Sofia: Medicina and Fitzcultura, 1973).

39 Ibid., 72.

40 Ibid., 72–6.

41 M. Lafrance, What's the Problem? *Canadian Issues* 1:1 (1999), 22; Nike web site, http://www.nike.com/jumpman23/index.html

42 A. Narvaez, The Fiftieth Anniversary of Women's Participation in Olympic Athletics, *Olympic Review* 134 (1978), 701.

43 M. C. Duncan, Gender Warriors in Sport, in A. Raney and J. Bryant (eds), *Handbook of Sports and Media* (Mahwah, NJ: Lawrence Erlbaum Associates, 2006), 231–52.

44 E. Trangbaek, Danish Women Gymnasts: An Olympic Success Story, *Olympic Perspectives* (October 1996), 237–44.

45 Cited ibid., 240.

46 L. Huntsman, *Sand in Our Souls* (Melbourne: Melbourne University Press, 2001).

47 V. Raszeja, *A Decent and Proper Exertion: The Rise of Women's Competitive Swimming in Sydney to 1912* (Australian Society for Sports History, Faculty of Arts and Social Sciences, University of Western Sydney, 1992).

48 Rose Scott quote in Randwick City Council historical exhibit, *Come in for a Swim: Mina Wylie*, Bowen Library, Maroubra, New South Wales (May–October, 2012).

49 Scott quoted in Guttmann, *The Olympics*, 33.

50 H. Lenskyj, *Out of Bounds: Women, Sport and Sexuality* (Toronto: Women's Press, 1986), 68–71.

51 See two of Guttmann's references to Scott: *The Olympics*, 33, and *Sports: The First Five Millennia* (Amherst MA: University of Massachusetts Press, 2007), 264; Scott, Rose (1847–1925), *Australian Dictionary of Biography*, http://adb. anu.edu.au/biography/scott-rose-8370

52 Guttmann, *The Olympics*, 32.

53 Raszeja, 68.

54 C. Colwin, *Breakthrough Swimming* (Champaign IL: Human Kinetics, 2002), 202; L. Borish, Charlotte Epstein, *Jewish Women: A Comprehensive Historical Encyclopedia*, Jewish Women's Archive, http://jwa.org/encyclopedia/article/ epstein-charlotte

DOI: 10.1057/9781137291158

55 H. Lenskyj, Olympic Power, Olympic Politics: Behind the Scenes, in A. Bairner and G. Molnar (eds), *The Politics of the Olympics* (London: Routledge, 2010), 24–5.
56 DeFranz; A. Blue, *Faster, Higher, Further: Women's Triumphs and Disasters at the Olympics* (London: Virago, 1988); S. Bandy, Politics of Gender through the Olympics, in Bairner and Molnar, 41–57.
57 N. Rosol cited in T. Terret, From Alice Milliat to Marie-Therese Eyquem: Revisiting Women's Sport in France (1920s–1960s), *International Journal of the History of Sport* 27:7 (2010), 1154–72.
58 A. Miragaya and L. DaCosta, Olympic Entrepreneurs – Alice Milliat: The 1st Woman Olympic Entrepreneur, Autonomous University of Barcelona Center for Olympic Studies web site, http://olympicstudies.uab.es/brasil/pdf/8.pdf
59 K. Wamsley and G. Schultz, Rogues and Bedfellows: The IOC and the Incorporation of the FSFI, in K. Wamsley et al. (eds), *Bridging Three Centuries*, Proceedings of the Fifth International Symposium for Olympic Research (London, ON: University of Western Ontario, 2000), 113–18.
60 *Official Bulletin of the International Olympic Committee* (April 2, 1926), 13.
61 Milliat cited in Terret, 1163.
62 Participation of Women in the Olympic Games, *Official Bulletin of the International Olympic Committee* 28 (May 1935).
63 British Olympic runner Harold Abrahams quoted in DeFranz, 187.
64 Wamsley and Schultz, 115.
65 M. Leigh and T. Bonin, The Pioneering Role of Madame Alice Milliat and the FSFI, *Journal of Sport History* 4:1 (1977), 72–83.
66 I. Buchanan, Asia's First Female Olympian, *Journal of Olympic History* (September 2000), 23–4.
67 H. Lenskyj, "We Want to Play, We'll Play": Women and Sport in the Twenties and Thirties, *Canadian Women's Studies* 4:3 (1983), 15–18.
68 T. Louis-Jacques, Black History Month: Louise Stokes, Malden Patch web site (February 14, 2012), http://malden.patch.com/articles/black-history-month-louise-stokes-fraser
69 E. Kjeldsen, Integration of Minorities into Olympic Sport in Canada and the USA, *Journal of Sport and Social Issues* 8:2 (1984), 30–44.
70 Associated Press and Grolier Enterprises, 131.
71 Warren, 168–82.
72 Babe Didrikson Zaharias's Legacy Fades, http://www.nytimes.com/2011/06/26/sports/golf/babe-didrikson-zahariass-legacy-fades.html?pagewanted=all
73 Caster Semenya Unveils Glamorous Look, Pink News web site (September 9, 2009), http://www.pinknews.co.uk/2009/09/09/caster-semenya-unveils-glamorous-look-as-she-learns-shell-keep-gold-medal/

DOI: 10.1057/9781137291158

74 F. Cosentino and G. Leyshon, *Olympic Gold* (Toronto: Holt, Rinehart and Winston, 1975).

75 M. Stell, *Half the Race: A History of Australian Women in Sport* (North Ryde, NSW: HarperCollins, 1992), 106.

76 Cited ibid., 258.

77 J. Levy, D. Rosenburg, and D. Hyman, Fanny "Bobbie" Rosenfeld: Canada's Woman Athlete of the Half Century, *Journal of Sport History* 26:2 (1999), 394, 395.

78 R. Fulford quoted in B. Macfarlane, Greatest Female Hockey Player of the 1920s, It Happened in Hockey web site (October 2009), http://www. ithappenedinhockey.com/2009/10/greatest-female-hockey-player-of-the-1920s/

79 Fanny Blankers-Koen, *Encyclopedia of World Biography* (2004), http://www. encyclopedia.com/topic/Fanny_Blankers-Koen.aspx

80 Stell, 119.

81 Ibid., 258.

82 Ibid., 195.

83 See, for example, R. Espy, *The Politics of the Olympic Games* (Berkeley CA: University of California Press, 1979); D. Rowe and G. Lawrence, Nationalism and the Olympics, in D. Rowe and G. Lawrence (eds), *Power Play* (Sydney: Iremonger, 1986), 196–203.

84 *Olympic Charter #57* (Lausanne: IOC, 2011).

85 L. Paradis, Manly Displays: Exhibitions and the Revival of the Olympic Games, *International Journal of the History of Sport* 27: 16–18 (2010), 2720–1.

86 Ibid., 2726.

87 Associated Press and Grolier Enterprises, 108.

88 From Hollywood Gold to Hollywood Glitters, *Olympic Review* 25:2 (1995), 50.

89 See, for example, Guttmann, *Sports*; R. Mandell, *The Nazi Olympics* (Chicago, IL: University of Illinois Press, 1971); Large.

90 G. Gori, "A Glittering Icon of Fascist Femininity": Trebisonda "Ondina" Valla, *International Journal of the History of Sport* 18:1 (2001), 173–95.

91 Guttmann, *Sports*; M. Dyreson, Johnny Weissmuller and the Old Global Capitalism: The Origins of the Federal Blueprint for Selling American Culture to the World, *International Journal of the History of Sport* 25:2 (2008), 268–83.

92 Dyreson, Johnny Weissmuller, 277.

93 From Hollywood Gold to Hollywood Glitters, 50–4.

94 Nendel; Cosentino and Leyshon.

95 La Guardia cited in M. Dyreson, From Civil Rights to Scientific Racism: The Variety of Responses to the Berlin Olympics, the Legend of Jesse Owens and the "Race Question," in R. Barney and K. Meier (eds), *Critical Reflections on Olympic Ideology*, Proceedings of the Second International Symposium for Olympic Research (London, ON: University of Western Ontario), 50.

DOI: 10.1057/9781137291158

96 J. Carlos with D. Zirin, *The John Carlos Story* (Chicago, IL: Haymarket Books, 2011).
97 In 1972, in a less publicized sequel, African American medallists Vince Matthews and Wayne Collett refused to stand at attention during the American national anthem, and were banned from further competition. See S. Russell, The Sydney 2000 Olympics and the Game of Political Repression: An Insider's Account, *Canadian Law and Society Association Bulletin* 18 (Fall 1994), 9–12.
98 Carlos, 113.
99 Owens quoted in Carlos, xv.
100 Foreman cited in Rowe and Lawrence, 199.
101 Carlos, xx.
102 T. Katz, panel discussion at *The Olympic Athlete* symposium, University of Toronto (April 4, 2012).
103 H. Edwards, *Sociology of Sport* (Belmont CA: Dorsey Press, 1973), 233.
104 See, for example, S. Cahn, *Coming on Strong: Gender and Sexuality in Twentieth-Century Women's Sport* (Cambridge, MA: Harvard University Press, 1994); M. A. Hall, *The Girl and the Game* (Toronto: University of Toronto Press, 2002); Lenskyj, *Out of Bounds*; J. Mangan and R. Park (eds), *From Fair Sex to Feminism* (London: Cass, 1987).
105 Kjeldsen. These are not the actual figures for teams that participated, since the US boycotted the 1980 Olympics. Kjeldsen cited as his source the *1980 Olympic Yearbook* published by the US Olympic Committee in 1981, which listed those who qualified for the US team.
106 From Hollywood Gold to Hollywood Glitters.
107 Role on TV "Tarzan" Makes Rafer Johnson a Bad Guy, *Baltimore Afro-American* (July 19, 1966), http://news.google.com/newspapers?nid=2205&dat=19660719&id=K8IlAAAAIBAJ&sjid=HPUFAAAAIBAJ&pg=988,3439270

DOI: 10.1057/9781137291158

5
In the Pool, on the Ice: Contested Terrain

Abstract: *From the earliest Olympic Games, the bodies of skaters and swimmers were gendered, raced and sexualized, with media coverage playing a key role in these processes. Debates about appearance, attire and comportment are central to questions of identity construction and the swimming and skating body. The Gay Games provide a compelling case study of a counter-hegemonic sporting event, and reveal some of the contradictions in Olympic sport.*

Lenskyj, Helen Jefferson. *Gender Politics and the Olympic Industry.* Basingstoke: Palgrave Macmillan, 2013. DOI: 10.1057/9781137291158.

In this chapter, I focus on two spaces, the swimming pool and the ice rink, that are well suited to an analysis of gender politics and the Olympic industry. Beginning with an historical overview, I look at the ways in which skaters and swimmers were gendered, raced and sexualized, with media coverage playing a key role in these processes. Debates about appearance, attire and comportment are central to questions of identity construction and the swimming and skating body. Finally, the Gay Games provide a compelling case study of a counter-hegemonic sporting event, and reveal some of the contradictions that abound in these sports.

There is a second reason for my choice of swimming: it is one of my favourite recreational sports. Sport scholars who are critical of the Olympics are often accused of simply not *liking* Olympic sport, even having a "passionate distaste" for it and an "inability to understand sporting passion."[1] While not supporting this kind of accusation, I can say that I do understand swimming passion.

In the pool

From sidestroke to crawl

Developments in swimming strokes provide an illuminating example of colonialism. In the 19th and early 20th centuries, sidestroke was the dominant swimming style in Europe, England, Canada and the US. At an 1844 exhibition in London, spectators were shocked by the "grotesque" style of two Ojibway men who swam using a version of what is now known as the crawl: "totally unEuropean" was one commentator's damning description.[2]

In 1873, John Trudgen, a British swimmer, introduced an overarm stroke that he had learned from Indigenous people of South America, later termed the "Indian stroke." Although this stroke proved superior to the more "refined" European and English styles that male swimmers adopted – "graceful and elegant movements, with a minimum of splashing," as swimming historian Cecil Colwin described them – the overarm or crawl stroke did not gain widespread popularity for several decades.[3]

In the early 1900s, Dick Cavill, an Australian swimmer, raced a very fast Samoan woman who used an overarm style but did not kick. He subsequently adopted a straight-leg kick that a Pacific Islander swimmer had learned from Native people in Ceylon (now Sri Lanka). After further experimentation, he developed the so-called Australian crawl, which,

DOI: 10.1057/

given its origins, should more accurately be called the "*Indigenous peoples' crawl*." Australian swimmer Fanny Durack switched from the trudgen to a version of the crawl in 1911, and proceeded to win every race over her Australian opponent Mina Wylie, who until that time had beaten her.

Modest attire for the ladies

The question of appropriate swimwear for women, a topic already introduced in Chapter 4, commanded public and media attention throughout the 20th century. Until the early 1900s, it was customary in most western countries for women to swim in a swimming dress, only slightly shorter than street clothes of the day, with stockings and shoes – in other words, they swam fully clothed. When wet, the outfit weighed up to 22 pounds.[4] Heavy, neck-to-knee woollen suits with a modesty "skirt" (an extra layer of fabric across the front) were followed in the 1920s by a similar style in cotton knit (yet another fabric that sagged when wet) that was developed by Speedo, at that time an Australian company.

From 1916 on, American and Australian knitting mills capitalized on the popularity of women's swimming, changing their original mundane company names to catchier ones such as Speedo, Cole of California, Catalina, and Jantzen ("The Suit that Changed Bathing to Swimming").[5] Further developments in nylon and elasticized fabrics led to more streamlined suits that reduced drag, culminating in the full-length bodysuits that the International Swimming Federation (FINA) approved for swimmers at the Sydney 2000 Olympics. These suits were banned in 2009 following debates over the validity of records achieved by swimmers who wore them. Almost 100 years earlier, Australian professional swimmer Annette Kellerman had been advocating for women's right to wear a form-fitting, full-length bodysuit with short sleeves, a style remarkably similar to the high-tech version of 2000, and equally controversial. Interestingly, between 2000 and 2009, the bodysuit had an unintended positive consequence for the women of Pakistan's national swim team, since it satisfied the Islamic dress requirement that women's bodies should be covered.[6]

Australian swimmer Mina Wylie wore a lightweight, sleeveless swimsuit made of silk and imported from England, its less restrictive style probably giving her an advantage over other swimmers.[7] Photographs of Wylie and Fanny Durack in 1912, posing proudly for the camera in their wet swimsuits, bring to mind the title of a 2010 article, "How to Look Good (Nearly) Naked".[8] On the basis of her research on UK swimmers

DOI: 10.1057/

in 2009, Susie Scott introduced the concept of "performative regulation" in relation to the swimmers' individual and social bodies. As she demonstrated, "The near-naked state of the swimmer's body presents a potential threat to the interaction order, insofar as social encounters may be misconstrued as sexual, and so rituals are enacted to create a 'civilized' definition of the situation."[9] In the very different social context of the early 1900s, similar rituals may have smoothed the way for female swimmers. For example, at the 1912 Stockholm Olympics, Durack and Wylie wore green caps and green cloaks over their swimming costumes until they began their races, thereby conforming to the new official dress code for female swimmers.[10] In a photograph of the 1912 Australasian (combined Australian and New Zealand) Olympic team, the two women are shown wearing bulky bathrobe-style coats bearing the team logo, as well as long white dresses, while the men wore regular attire with team jackets.[11] Until at least the 1920s, female tennis players at Wimbledon and the Olympics attracted criticism when they wore dresses with short sleeves that revealed bare forearms (although they retained the prerequisite white stockings), while female swimmers pioneered functional swimsuit styles that eventually became more widely accepted.

Weighing in on women's Olympic sport in 1936, Finnish runner Paavo Nurmi pronounced swimming acceptable, but called for events such as javelin and high jump to be "forbidden" on the grounds that he "could not bear to watch [women] … contorting [and] convulsing" their bodies. He went on to explain that he admired the Dutch women swimmers, because "Such contests do not prevent women from remaining ladies."[12]

By the 1980s, however, the evolution of high performance sport had led to specialized training programmes and a selection process based on optimal body types, producing female swimmers who would not have satisfied this conservative view of "ladies." Nor did female swimmers' bodies meet contemporary definitions of "feminine" in western society. Former Olympic swimmer Nikki Dryden recalled how she saw herself in high school: "I knew I wasn't looking the same way as other young girls … [so] I became punk, dyed my hair, cut it short, I took it to extremes … away from femininity."[13]

It is possible, of course, that male authorities' constant references to the "beauty and grace" of the "ladies" in the pool concealed men's underlying interest in admiring female bodies wearing considerably less clothing than most women of the day – thereby confirming Guttmann's theories on the *eros*/sport connection. As noted earlier, the women in sport administration who objected to male audiences certainly believed that voyeurism was men's prime motive. In the same vein, they wanted girls and women to have female coaches and trainers, a difficult goal to achieve in a period when career paths for women in sport were limited.

That situation had not changed significantly by the end of the 20th century, largely on account of structural barriers. Competing at the national and internationals level in the 1990s, Dryden pointed out that almost all the coaches and support staff were men, with the possible exception of a female manager and "mother figure."[14] She noted that there were more female coaches in the NCAA, and that these women, successful swimmers themselves, could coach at the college level rather than start off in age-group coaching (children and adolescents), a job that required travelling and working on weekends and thus presented obstacles for many women, especially those with children.

The swimmer's body: inappropriate touching

Until the late 1980s, sexual harassment and sexual abuse in sport were rarely recognized or documented, and sport scholars were just beginning to address these issues.[15] The perpetrators were mostly male coaches, and their targets were mostly girls and young women, and sometimes boys. How widespread the problems were before western feminist activists raised public awareness of abuse issues outside sport, and eventually within sport, is impossible to calculate. For many decades, there were reports of various kinds of physical abuse of young athletes in former Eastern Bloc countries, with the East German state-ordered doping policy, discussed below, representing the most serious example. As recently as 2004, reports from China, where an estimated two-thirds of the country's professional athletes were children, documented "inhumane" training methods and sexual abuse.[16] This is not to suggest that sporting practices in western countries always hold to higher ethical standards in relation to child athletes.[17]

A widespread problem in western countries as well as Eastern Europe was the kind of psychological abuse by male coaches that produced eating disorders – anorexia and bulimia. This abuse included daily public weigh-ins in an era when "it was okay to call girls fat," as Dryden explained. The problem was first recognized in the 1980s and was well documented among girls and women in sports such as gymnastics, where thinness was seen as contributing to winning performances, but

DOI: 10.1057/

less thoroughly investigated in other sports. By the end of the 1990s in western countries, more effective measures were in place to train coaches and monitor coaching practices in order to prevent eating disorders, but other problems in coach–athlete relationships remained.

Swimming presents specific opportunities for both appropriate and inappropriate touching because of the nature of the sport, coaching styles and the exposed body of the swimmer. A 2003 controversy in Australian high performance swimming circles uncovered the common and largely unquestioned coaching behaviours of the 1980s. Two female swimmers accused their male coaches, Scott Volkers and Greg Hodge, of sexual misconduct. Charges were dropped against Volkers; the Hodge case went to court, the swimmer lost, and Hodge successfully sued for damages on the grounds of defamation. The mainstream media's attempts at investigative journalism demonstrate their power to shape the discourse.

By 2003, both Volkers and Hodge were coaching national teams, and the 2004 Athens Olympics were less than a year away – not a convenient time for Australia to lose its top coaches. Since the accusations referred back to events of the 1980s and 1990s, journalists sought out retired female swimmers and coaches in a transparent attempt to support the position that "everyone was doing it" back in the day. That is, all the male coaches were giving full-body massages ("rub-downs") to young female and male swimmers, because at this time, teams did not have massage therapists – and it was "innocent." In Canada, too, Dryden recalled some "touchy-feely" swim coaches in the 1990s, and, again, "everybody knew." She also noted that going to the coach's hotel room "to talk about race strategy" was a routine practice.

Former Australian national coach Don Talbot admitted that "a lot of people" were uncomfortable with the "rub-down" practice: the young swimmers, male and female, the coaches and the parents. He also acknowledged that the practice gave abusers "a foot in the door" by legitimizing touching of swimmers' bodies. However, former swimmers lined up to support Hodge and Volkers, and to validate the coaching practices of the 1980s and 1990s. Significantly, there was little if any support for the two women who made the allegations, or for other victims who had remained silent.

"I never, never found it was crossing the line of touchy-feely type things," said Michelle Ford, while Tracey Wickham, another 1980s champion, claimed that all coaches did what Hodge did: "fixing straps up, giving them a hug or kiss ... patting them on the back," thereby skirting the real issue of *sexual* touching. Several swimmers and coaches expressed

DOI: 10.1057/

more concern about the "damage" to the sport and the coaching profession, claiming that male coaches were leaving swimming because of worries about false accusations.[18]

A few recommended "common sense," noting that coaches needed to be more aware of boundaries, and to adhere to the Australian swimming code of conduct, which specifically named "inappropriate intimacy" between coach and athlete as "sexual misconduct." Another provision stated that no person should "touch anyone in a way that makes them feel uncomfortable," thereby putting the responsibility for defining "uncomfortable" on the (child or adolescent) athlete rather than the (adult) coach.[19] Furthermore, coaching methods in sports such as gymnastics, swimming and diving typically involve hands-on demonstrations and/ or spotting, and cultural differences between coaches and athletes shape perceptions of appropriate and inappropriate touching. Viewing television coverage of Olympic events, one can see cultural differences played out in the range of interactions between coaches and athletes following successful or unsuccessful performances. The "different culture" excuse does not, of course, justify unethical behaviour on the part of coaches.

A scene that has remained with me for many years took place during women's gymnastics at the 1996 Atlanta Olympics: the actions of Márta Károlyi, wife of Romanian coach Béla Károlyi, both of whom were at that time coaching the US women's team. After one gymnast had performed poorly and was walking back to the bench, Márta put her hand on the back of the girl's neck in what appeared to be a comforting gesture, then squeezed her neck and gave her a slight push. Since this took place in front of dozens of television cameras and millions of viewers, it raises serious questions concerning coaching practices behind closed doors.

On the issue of sexual harassment, Dryden identified another under-recognized problem that she experienced as a member of the Canadian national team in the 1990s: sexual harassment at the hands of male peers. Unlike club teams, the national team included several very young female swimmers – she was 14, while most of her male teammates were in their late teens, "very sexually active" and, on occasion, sexually aggressive. Further adding to the dangers of this situation, after the competition, "everyone was drinking and partying," including underage swimmers and their coaches, and "no one ever talked about it, or warned you." These practices ended abruptly after 1992 when six swimmers on the national team were kicked out of the Olympic Village following "high jinks." A new rule applied to swimmers in the 1996 Olympics: "No sex, no drugs, no alcohol."

DOI: 10.1057/

Doping and swimming

Between 1972 and 1989, the German Democratic Republic implemented a policy of administering performance-enhancing drugs to athletes in government-sponsored elite sport schools. Of the thousands of athletes involved, most were under the age of 16 and were not told the purpose of the drugs, while those over 18 had to sign an oath of secrecy. Coaches and doctors were brought to trial in 1998, found guilty of bodily harm and administering drugs to minors, and given relatively small fines and/or suspended sentences. Hundreds of these young athletes subsequently developed physical and mental health problems, and some sought compensation in the courts.

German women, unrivalled swimming champions for more than 25 years, were the best-known products of the state doping policy. Some of these women testified against their coaches and subsequently told their stories to the media. In addition to the virilizing effects of steroids, there were serious health outcomes, including liver cancer and infertility, and some of these women had children with birth defects.[20]

Chinese swimmers, almost all female, made dramatic improvements between the 1988 and 1996 Olympics, and their performances, as well as their impressive muscularity, prompted coaches to pressure FINA to introduce a more thorough and effective drug-testing programme. By 2000, 38 Chinese swimmers had tested positive for drugs, well ahead of the next country, Russia (USSR) with 8.[21]

Obstacles: class and race

The benefits of swimming, generally framed in terms of health and social control, have been widely recognized since the late 1800s. Opportunities for working-class families expanded over the course of the 20th century as European workers' sport organizations and YWCAs, YMCAs and YWHAs around the world offered classes to all ages in indoor pools. Single-sex organizations avoided potential problems involving appropriate apparel, but boys and young men continued to have more freedom and hence more opportunities for swimming outdoors – in rivers, lakes and the ocean – than girls and women.

As the sport developed at the high performance level, the demands of training presented obstacles for working-class and ethnic minority swimmers in western countries. Systemic racism in the US, combined with social-economic inequalities, produced often insurmountable barriers

DOI: 10.1057/

for African American families. Before the changes brought about by the 1960s civil rights movement, public pools barred the entry of Black swimmers, and they were unlikely to be able to afford fees for expensive country clubs, if indeed they were accepted as members. Even after the 1960s, innercity neighbourhoods where working-class Black families lived were unlikely to have well-maintained public pools, nor did their local high schools. And, as author Philip Hoose pointed out, "the private club is the foundation of American competitive swimming."[22] That, as well as all the other expenses associated with meets, makes it a sport that is out of the reach of working-class families.

As a five-year-old in 1948, Chris Silva, who later became the first Black swimmer on the US national team, experienced the racism of that era when he was the only Black child taking part in a swimming clinic in Long Beach. His mother recalled that he was treated as an oddity because of his skin colour and his hair. A white man at the pool announced to all present (inaccurately, since Silva was an excellent swimmer) that the "heavy bones" of Black people meant that they were unable to swim.[23]

Numerous other myths abounded concerning the Black body's alleged inability to swim or float, for the most part based on racist, pseudo-scientific hearsay involving bone density, fast- and slow-twitch muscle ratio and so on. This kind of misinformation about Black swimmers continues, to a lesser extent, today, in reference not only to African Americans but to Black populations throughout the world. A Google search, "why no Black swimmers in Olympics," generated countless results, with references to alleged physiological differences and deficits still surfacing in some of these sources. Significantly, the question does not appear to have generated the volume of racist research that was prompted by the *success* of Black athletes, presumably because white scientists and the white sport world are more interested in Black winners than Black "losers." The fact that increasing numbers of Black athletes are competing in swimming at the international level reveals the flaws in physiology-based explanations.

From water ballet to synchronized swimming

Australian professional swimmer Annette Kellerman, famed for her English Channel swims in the early 1900s, has sometimes been credited as the originator of water ballet, later called synchronized swimming, although American Esther Williams is more universally recognized as the pioneer, no doubt because of her high profile in film.

DOI: 10.1057/

While it shares many features with ballet and figure skating, where men and women perform together, synchronized swimming is, strangely, a predominantly female sport, having women's pairs and team events, although there is greater participation and acceptance of male synchro swimmers in Europe than in other western countries. The Gay Games, of course, include competitions for men as well as women, but no men, gay or straight, have that opportunity in the Olympics. In 2000, FINA accepted male/female pairs in international competition, but the federation did not push for mixed pairs' inclusion in the 2004 Olympic programme, and it has remained excluded.

The few American men who have competed in synchro swimming since 2000 continue to attract widespread media and public attention, both positive and negative, with Bill May and Kenyon Smith among the best-known male representatives of the sport. Ironically, much of the coverage echoes themes that were central in earlier decades when women began participating in non-traditional (male) sports. Journalists routinely ask these men how they got interested, what attracted them to the sport and whether they have experienced any negative reactions. Many say they belonged to swim clubs as children, had sisters in synchro, watched them practising and then became interested themselves. Some were harassed as children, and some experienced occasional audience hostility as adults; others no doubt dropped out because of harassment.

The most salient problem that they identified was the "gay stigma," and their most common reaction was remarkably similar to the "female apologetic" of the 1970s in women's sport: repeated affirmations of their heterosexual identity. Smith was quoted in a newspaper article as saying, "I'm the one who gets to hang out with a group of girls in bikinis every day," but he assured readers that he did not date the women on his team, adding nobly, "I've had to break some hearts, unfortunately."[24] Bill May, presenting more of a metrosexual image, was reported to enjoy gourmet cooking.

When Bill May and female partner Kristina Lum competed in the pairs competition at the Goodwill Games in 1998, one commentator praised their "steamy, ground-breaking performance to Ravel's 'Bolero,'" in which they appeared to be channelling British ice dancers Torvill and Dean. As Lum explained, "we really tried to play off the passion between a man and a woman."[25]

Commenting on the interest shown by Chinese officials after seeing the pair at the Goodwill Games, their coach, Chris Carver, expressed her admiration for the Chinese approach to sport: "They don't have the

DOI: 10.1057/

cultural roadblocks we do," she said. "They'll just take all the little boys out of villages and *make them do it* – kind of like they do with diving" (emphasis added).[26] This attitude on the part of an American coach (or indeed any coach) is disturbing, although those who have been acculturated into the world of Olympic sport may disagree. Indeed, officials in high performance sport institutes in liberal-democratic countries, including Canada, the US and Australia, select children and adolescents with athletic potential and often take them out of their homes for intense training, all in the name of Olympic medals and national pride.

Gina Arnold, one of the journalists who interviewed Carver and May, elaborated on the gay stigma. In a telling example of the social construction of heterosexuality, she explained,

> In America, the idea of men doing synchronised swimming seems positively gay – but in fact, strictly speaking, it is the opposite of gay. The sight of May and Lum performing to Ravel's "Bolero" is, frankly, a lot more *natural-looking* than the sight of two women mirroring one another's movements. (emphasis added)[27]

Yet the relatively new Olympic event of synchronized diving – for men and for women – has similar components, without necessarily attracting the homophobic "unnatural" stigma or assumptions that male (or female) divers are gay (although some are).

On the subject of male divers, an incident during the 2008 Beijing Olympics demonstrated some change in attitudes. When NBC reported on Australian Matthew Mitcham's gold medal win (remarkable in that he was the only non-Chinese diver, male or female, to win a gold medal at these Olympics), they failed to mention that he was gay and had a partner. When challenged about this omission, NBC went on at length about time limitations, privacy concerns and so on, although their web site had included the information that Mitcham was openly gay. The network eventually issued an apology for missing "the opportunity to tell Matthew Mitcham's story. We apologize for this unintentional omission."[28] As some critics noted, the *hetero*sexuality of Olympic athletes – Michael Phelps, for example – was clearly revealed during NBC interviews; hence their initial claim that they did not discuss athletes' sexual orientation was untrue.[29] That this remained a blind spot for NBC in 2008 was disturbing, but the fact that there was any controversy at all about NBC's omission reflects some positive change in media practices as a result of decades of LGBT activism.

DOI: 10.1057/

Journalist Gina Arnold claimed that the "plastic grin" on the face of a female swimmer is readily accepted, while on a male swimmer it would look "phony." Presumably a smiling woman (even with noseclips and Vaselined hair) symbolizes hegemonic femininity. After all, the managed smile has come to be expected of women who provide entertainment and services for men – from flight attendants to sex trade workers.

In displays that are more ironic than serious, the men who compete in synchro in the Gay Games have the prerequisite smiles, along with the sequins and shaved legs. Illustrating the arbitrariness of body grooming behaviours, competitive male cyclists and swimmers also shave their legs, but when male synchro swimmers do so for image rather than functional reasons, the same result is read as effeminate. And when newspaper photographs of East German swimmer Cornelia Ender at the 1976 Montreal Olympics showed that she had underarm hair as well as large quads, that "masculine" image alone implied steroid use.[30]

Further musing on the inclusion of men in synchro, Arnold predicted that athleticism would become more prominent and that the sport would "start getting respect." It seems more likely that men's participation will add more obvious heteronormative content to the routines rather than downplaying appearance and promoting athleticism. In the 1980s, when some women tried to persuade synchro officials to allow them to wear regular swimsuits and caps, they were unsuccessful.

Carver, the synchro coach, went on to say, "There's a whole new aspect with males ... It's a lot like the pairs in figure skating. There's a lot of interplay, a lot of high lifts that are not there with the (women-only) duets. It's all very exciting." One might ask why, if the women's pairs appear so "unnatural," so lacking in interplay, athleticism and excitement, the women-only sport is so popular. The fact that May received the US Synchronized Swimming Athlete of the Year award in 1998 suggests that different criteria were applied to males and females, because his part of the routine, as in figure skating or ballet, was quite different from a woman's: he did the high lifts, for example.

On the ice

Men, women and skates

Female figure skaters have outnumbered men on the ice, and outperformed them in terms of sponsorships, since the 1930s. Before that time,

DOI: 10.1057/

it was a predominantly male activity, particularly in England and Europe, but with significant differences in style. European influences eventually prevailed, and, as Mary Louise Adams explained in her comprehensive history of the sport, "To prove their mettle, English skaters had to temper their manly reserve, adopt a more expressive style, and skate like 'effete' Continentals."[31] This was probably the same "manly reserve" that caused British spectators to be shocked by the swimming performances of the two Native North American men described earlier. By the 1980s, the notion of "effete" had taken on homophobic dimensions, as the lyrical styles and fancy costumes of male figure skaters came to be interpreted as gay.

Sonja Henie popularized the sport for women following her performances at the Olympics in 1928, 1932 and 1936, and, of course, her Hollywood career. However, unlike men's figure skating, which has evolved in a range of ways – from lyrical to macho and back – in different countries and different historical periods, women's figure skating continues to reflect the legacy of Henie's ultra-feminine style. As Adams concluded, "figure skating continues to support and reward only a limited range of intransigently traditional femininities, none of which foreground women's strength and power... Female figure skaters are almost always positioned as elegant princesses, bubbly pixies or alluring vixens."[32] Of course, this positioning is the result of a complex system, as choreographers and coaches shape female skaters whose technical and artistic skills will win points, and whose image will entertain audiences and attract sponsorships, and the dominant image is that of white femininity. As a *Ms.* magazine journalist observed in 1994, the sport is "puritanical" and the women "have to be clean-cut, wholesome and virginal." At that time, American Tonya Harding was the only married woman who had performed singles skating in the Olympics.[33]

The whiteness of ice and snow sports

Only a small minority of Olympic figure skaters, male or female, are Black, Hispanic or South Asian. As with swimming, tennis, golf and similar sports, this is largely an outcome of the combined effects of racism and classism. To rise to top levels in these sports requires membership in private clubs and considerable investments in time and money, which poses barriers to children in most working-class, Black, Hispanic and immigrant families.

DOI: 10.1057/

Furthermore, winter sports have long been a predominantly white preserve as a result of systemic barriers as well as racist assumptions that "geography is destiny." Analysing this aspect of the Winter Olympics, I found a favourite rationale for these sports' whiteness was geography: athletes from warm or temperate climates, it is claimed, are at a geographic disadvantage because they don't have access to year-round ice and snow. But no one argues that athletes from cold climates, lacking year-round access to outdoor fields, tracks, roads, mountains or beaches, suffer a geographic disadvantage.[34] If geography were the key factor, Northern European athletes, for example, would be expected not to have much success in summer sports. But in fact, athletes from western countries, warm and cold, have had high medal counts in Summer and Winter Olympics throughout most of the 20th century, and athletes from colder countries have outperformed those from warmer countries even in sports of the Summer Games, a trend that is in large part attributable to economic and political determinants.[35] In short, geography is not a barrier in countries that have the financial resources to compensate for any disadvantages posed by climate or in countries that have the greatest political investment in producing medal-winning performances every two years to gain sporting ascendancy on the world stage.

Sexism and homophobia on ice

Although men's individual figure skating allows for, perhaps encourages, the kind of flamboyancy often associated with gay male celebrities, the choreography of the pairs figure skating and ice dancing programmes counters this trend, as does the ruling against same-sex pairs competitions in international ice skating (with the notable exception of the Gay Games). In pairs figure skating and ice dancing, heteronormativity is announced in every move, with sexual attraction and tension between the two partners playing a key role in their performance, as synchro swimmer Kristina Lum pointed out. This posed a challenge for the many brother-and-sister pairs who competed in international figure skating competition, particularly when they performed the unequivocally heterosexy tango, which became a compulsory component of ice dancing in 1976. Some brother–sister pairs avoided the problem by performing nonsexual, humorous routines, but most simply recognized that they needed to act the part, and seemed to assume that the audience would forget that they were siblings and focus on their performance.[36]

DOI: 10.1057/

Both male and female figure skaters face a range of sexist and homophobic stereotypes: the women are expected to be graceful and beautiful, while the men are assumed to be gay – and in this context, gay is not good. In 2009, Skate Canada identified a problem of decreasing numbers of boys taking up the sport. They urged coaches and athletes to promote a more "masculine" skating style and to work at attracting more of "an ice hockey crowd"[37] – a curious goal in view of the sanctioned, crowd-pleasing violence of the National Hockey League in the US and Canada.

Canadian Elvis Stojko had pioneered a more "butch" style of men's figure skating and costuming in the 1990s, to counter the so-called effeminacy trend. A Toronto journalist's commentary on his 1997 televised special, *Elvis Incognito*, gives some indication of his challenge to the "sequins-and-glitter" image of male figure skaters: "a multifaceted character who unveils himself during the show … having Elvis drive a motorcycle, lip synch an arena rock anthem … and hold forth cryptically on the benefits of martial arts."[38]

Just before the 2010 Vancouver Winter Olympics, Stojko called for greater emphasis on "masculinity, strength and power" in men's skating. "People in the gay community have to realize they've got to take themselves out of it," he added – not because he was "against anybody," but because, he claimed, people couldn't identify with "effeminate" performances, and the future of the sport was under threat. Like the Australian swimming coaches discussed earlier, Stojko expressed greater feeling and sensitivity towards "the sport" than towards the men, women and children who constitute it. This kind of discourse, common in the world of high performance sport, obliterates the human element as it reifies the institution.

Apart from the obvious offensiveness of his statement, Stojko seems to have overlooked the longstanding presence of (mostly closeted) gay men in figure skating, as coaches, choreographers and judges as well as skaters, and the fact that their performances had boosted its popularity significantly since the 1980s. In 1997, for example, the televised Canadian national championships attracted almost two million viewers over seven hours of prime-time coverage.[39] This is not to suggest that the sport of figure skating provided a welcoming climate for gay men or boys. After Canadian Brian Orser was outed through a palimony suit in 1998, he received public support, but no other skater came out as gay in solidarity with him.[40]

Rudy Galindo was the only figure skater to come out during his competitive career. Gay, working-class, Mexican American (and later HIV

DOI: 10.1057/

positive), he took a considerable risk doing so as he had already attracted negative attention from judges and audiences with his long hair, makeup and "feminine" costumes. In 1996, he was left off Skate America's team, and, as he wrote in his autobiography, his coach was convinced that the US Figure Skating Association (USFSA) "didn't want an effeminate gay man representing the United States at Skate America," the most prestigious international competition held in the US.[41] Discussing his Hispanic identity in a 2002 interview, Galindo said, "I think I was discriminated against my whole life in skating, practically. I had to work twice as hard and just make sure those judges had no excuse not to give me first or place me, at nationals or internationals."[42]

"Skating's tragic secret"

A chapter with this title in American sportswriter Christine Brennan's 1997 book *Inside Edge* discussed the dramatic impact of the AIDS crisis on everyone involved in figure skating at the national and international levels, including athletes, their partners and families, coaches, choreographers and judges. The "secret" referred to the silence surrounding AIDS deaths in the figure skating world of the 1980s and into the 1990s; a 1992 report estimated that the number of deaths among American and Canada skaters and coaches was at least 40. Yet, as Brennan explained, the USFSA was slow to respond because it saw this as a potential public relations disaster: "AIDS means homosexuality...How does the organization say it has lost more athletes to AIDS than any other sport in the country?"[43] To acknowledge the presence of gay men in figure skating would jeopardize sponsorships and TV ratings, and raise fears among parents. In addition to the Americans, the high-profile figure skaters who died of AIDS included John Curry from the UK, Ondrej Nepela from Czechoslovakia, and Rob McCall, Brian Pockar, Dennis Coi and Shaun McGill from Canada. The USFSA eventually held discussions and educational sessions on AIDS prevention for skaters and coaches.

"Bad examples" of masculinity?

In 2010, American Johnny Weir, whose gender-bending style made him a media magnet following the 2006 Torino Olympics, came out as gay, to no one's surprise, after having spent several years avoiding questions about his sexuality. During the 2010 Vancouver Olympics, two announcers on a Canadian sport channel made homophobic comments about

DOI: 10.1057/

Weir, claiming that he was a "bad example" for boys. Their so-called jokes included the suggestions that "We should make him pass a gender test" or "compete in the women's competition." Following a public outcry, the announcers and the television station issued apologies.[44] On a more positive note, when Weir married his partner in 2011, the mainstream media treated the event in much the same way that it treated hetero-sexual sport celebrities' marriages.

The year 1994 marked the first time that two men competed in the Gay Games figure skating pairs, in a routine that had the traditional lifts of opposite-sex pairs. Canadian skaters Jean-Pierre Martin and Mark Hird had first practised together in the Bell Amphitheatre in Montreal, where Martin worked as a consultant and ice-show producer. When his boss objected, the pair started practising at a suburban Montreal rink, again sparking "a flood of complaints from parents scandalised by Mr. Martin lifting and spinning Mr. Hird," as reported by journalist Andre Picard, who went on to identify the arbitrary standards that make ice hockey masculine:

> When 12 men skate together on the Montreal Forum ice, chasing a piece of hard black rubber and whacking each other for good measure, that's manly... But when Mr. Martin and Mr. Hird... spin and leap on the ice of the Bell Amphitheatre, the reaction is still decidedly cool, the recognition of their art... distant.[45]

When Martin and Hird invited CBC television cameras to follow their experiences, culminating in the documentary titled *Breaking Barriers*, the Bell people reversed their decision and offered them free training time. One account of these events noted that objections had been made on the grounds that the two men had been seen kissing, which they said was untrue. Furthermore, there were two mentions of the fact that Martin and Hird "were friends but not lovers."[46] The reason for this com-mentator's emphasis on their relationship status is unclear. After all, the homophobic response reflected moral outrage that two gay men would dare to perform a routine reserved for a heterosexual couple, and their relationship to each other was a side issue.

As in men's synchro swimming, there has long been a pattern in American and Canadian men's figure skating circles of "coming out straight" in the media: repeated assertions of heterosexuality through references to wives, girlfriends and children. Given the "gay stigma" that the sport attracts, there appears to be no place for the metrosexual man in figure skating. Conversely, in sports where all the men are assumed to

DOI: 10.1057/

be straight – basketball, baseball, football and ice hockey, for example – there is more scope for, and less threat to, players who fit the metrosexual image. These are men who devote an unusual (for a man) amount of attention to clothing, jewellery, personal appearance and each other's bodies – in the locker room, in the nude. John Amaechi, a Black basketball player and the first to come out as gay following his retirement from the National Basketball Association, discussed these practices in his 2007 autobiography *Man in the Middle*. As he explained, these exchanges, which included flaunting their "perfect bodies," reflected "an intense kind of camaraderie that felt completely natural to them but was a little too close for my comfort ... and I'm the gay one."[47] Amaechi reported an interesting cultural twist in gay stereotypes. Growing up in England, he had a British accent, and whenever there were questions about his (hetero)sexuality, "people would quip, 'Oh, he's just English. Leave him alone.'"[48]

At elite levels in women's sport, however, a different set of norms prevailed in many locker rooms. As Nikki Dryden observed, the majority of swimmers covered up their bodies, in and out of the showers, while some soccer players even showered in their sports bras. This is a pattern I've also observed for the past 20 years among women in the university's swim team. Nudity seems to be taboo, perhaps as a kind of defence against rumours of lesbianism. In the 1990s, when Dryden was competing, she faced homophobic accusations because of her short hair and her close friendship with a female swimmer with whom she trained. The rumours, started by male peers, ruined their friendship, an outcome that she continues to find upsetting. And, like other young women trying to find their identity, she found that "the only way to be feminine was to have sex" with these boys.

Conclusion

Throughout the history of the Olympics, the politics of sex, gender and sexuality have been played out in the pool and on the ice, as the arbitrary inclusions and exclusions of the Olympic programme reflected and reinforced gender binaries and heteronormativity. Unlike most male sports, men's figure skating displayed a level of "beauty and grace" traditionally reserved for female athletes, but this trend did not go unnoticed or unchallenged, as seen in recent moves to "masculinize" the sport. For their part, female figure skaters and synchro swimmers have had limited

DOI: 10.1057/

success in promoting athleticism and challenging hegemonic femininity. An alternative sporting festival, the Gay Games, has successfully countered some of these trends. In the next chapter, I continue to examine issues of sex and sexualities in the broader context of Olympic sport and the Olympic industry.

Notes

1 R. Cashman, Barrackers' Corner: A Rejoinder to a "One-Eyed" Review of *Staging the Olympics, Sporting Traditions* 18:1 (2001), 127–9. Cashman was reacting to Douglas Booth's well-argued critical review of *Staging the Olympics* (co-edited with Anthony Hughes) in an earlier issue of *Sporting Traditions*.

2 Cited in C. Colwin, *Breakthrough Swimming* (Champaign, IL: Human Kinetics, 2002), 14; see also P. Hoose, *Necessities: Racial Barriers in American Sports* (New York: Random House, 1989), 70.

3 Colwin, 3.

4 *Swimsuits: A Hundred Years of Pictures* (Washington DC: National Geographic Society, 2000).

5 Swimwear Historical Timeline, GlamourSurf web site, http://www.glamoursurf.com/swimwear_timeline.html

6 Interview with Nikki Dryden (Toronto, May 14, 2012).

7 Randwick City Council historical exhibit, *Come in for a Swim: Mina Wylie*, Bowen Library, Maroubra, New South Wales (May–October, 2012).

8 S. Scott, How to Look Good (Nearly) Naked: Regulation of the Swimmer's Body, *Body & Society* 16:2 (2010), 143–68.

9 Ibid., 143.

10 M. Stell, *Half the Race: A History of Australian Women in Sport* (North Ryde, NSW: HarperCollins, 1992), 159; *Come in for a Swim.*

11 Australasian Olympic team 1912 photograph, New South Wales State Library, in *Come in for a Swim.*

12 Nurmi quoted in Stell, 108.

13 Interview with Nikki Dryden.

14 Ibid.

15 When I began researching these issues in 1990, there were very few sources. The most important was Donald Lackey's study of sexual harassment experienced by female athletes at the hands of male coaches in American college and university sport; see D. Lackey, Sexual Harassment in Sports, *Physical Education* 47:2 (1990), 22–6.

16 F. Hong, Innocence Lost: Child Athletes in China, *Sport in Society* 7:3 (2004), 342.

DOI: 10.1057/

17   C. Breckenridge, *Spoilsports* (London: Routledge, 2001).

18   Swimming's Touchy Issue, *Sydney Morning Herald* (September 20, 2003); S. Meacham, Too Close for Comfort, *Sydney Morning Herald* (October 18, 2003), 36; R. Yallop, Intimacy and Betrayal, *The Australian* (October 23, 2003).

19   Swimming's Touchy Issue.

20   K. Volkwein, Sport and Ethics in Unified Germany – A Critical Analysis, in R. Barney and K. Meier (eds), Proceedings of the First International Symposium for Olympic Research (London, ON: University of Western Ontario, 1992), 55–66; Colwin.

21   Colwin, 215.

22   Hoose, 77.

23   Ibid., 74.

24   K. Melloy, No Olympic Glory for Male Synchronized Swimmers, *Edge Boston* (July 30, 2008), http://www.edgeboston.com/index.php?ch=news&sc=glbt&sc2=news&sc3=&id=78177

25   T. Ziemer, Out of Sync: Male Synchro Swimmer Banned from Olympics, ABC News web site, http://www.tracyziemer.com/ABC-NEWS-out-of-sync.htm

26   G. Arnold, Synch Different, *Metroactive* (September 10–16, 1998), http://www.metroactive.com/papers/metro/09.10.98/cover/synchroswim-9836.html

27   Ibid.

28   NBC Apologizes for Mitcham Gay Snub, OutSports web site (September 27, 2008), http://outsports.com/olympics2008/2008/08/27/nbc-apologizes-for-mitcham-gay-snub/

29   NBC Defends Not Saying Mitcham Is Gay, OutSports web site (September 25, 2008), http://outsports.com/olympics2008/2008/08/25/nbc-defends-not-saying-mitcham-is-gay/

30   D. Morrow, Olympic Masculinity, in K. Wamsley et al. (eds), *The Global Nexus Engaged*, Proceedings of the Sixth International Symposium for Olympic Research (London, ON: University of Western Ontario, 2002), 126.

31   M. L. Adams, *Artistic Impressions: Figure Skating, Masculinity, and the Limits of Sport* (Toronto: University of Toronto Press, 2011), 104.

32   Ibid., 199.

33   K. Rounds, Ice: Reflections on a Sport Out of Whack, *Ms.* (May/June 1994), 27. Harding was better known for her involvement in the attack on Nancy Kerrigan, in an attempt to eliminate her rival from upcoming competitions.

34   See H. Lenskyj, The Winter Olympics: Geography Is Destiny? in H. Lenskyj and S. Wagg (eds), *Handbook of Olympic Studies* (Basingstoke, UK: Palgrave Macmillan, 2012), 88–102.

35   D. Wallechinsky, *Complete Book of the Olympics* (Harmondsworth, UK: Penguin, 1984); D. Johnson and A. Ali, A Tale of Two Seasons, *Social Science Quarterly* 85:4 (2004), 974–93.

DOI: 10.1057/

36 S. James, Brother-Sister Skating Pairs, Too Close for Comfort, ABC News web site (February 19, 2010), http://abcnews.go.com/Health/Olympics/olympic-brother-sister-skating-pairs-close-vancouver-ice/story?id=9887494

37 T. Rogers, Can Figure Skating Go Butch? Salon.com web site (February 15, 2010), http://www.salon.com/2010/02/15/elvis_stojko_interview/

38 D. Bell, Figure Skating, the Never-Ending Story, *Globe and Mail* (February 8, 1997), D9.

39 Ibid.

40 Adams, 58.

41 R. Galindo, with E. Marcus, *Icebreaker* (New York: Pocket Books, 1997), 141; see also C. Brennan, *Inside Edge* (New York: Knopf Doubleday, 1997), 69.

42 K. Kaufman, So They're All Gay, Right? Salon.com web site (February 22, 2002), http://www.salon.com/2002/02/22/galindo/

43 Brennan, 57.

44 TV Crew Upsets Gay Rights Group, *Toronto Star* (February 21, 2010).

45 A. Picard, Skating with an Olympic-Sized Dream, *Globe and Mail* (February 15, 1994), A7.

46 M. Garber, Victor Petrenko's Mother-in-Law, in C. Baughmann (ed.), *Women on Ice* (New York: Routledge, 1995), 98.

47 D. Amaechi, *Man in the Middle* (New York: ESPN Books, 2007), 140.

48 Ibid., 271.

DOI: 10.1057/

6
Sex and the Games

Abstract: *This chapter examines issues relating specifically to sex and sport, with a focus on historical and contemporary constructions of and challenges to hegemonic sexual identities. Topics include performance-enhancing drugs, sexploitation of athletes' bodies and the IOC's gender verification processes, with special attention to the case of Caster Semenya. Other sex-related problems – sexual harassment perpetrated by male IOC members and street sweeps targeting sex trade workers and sexual minorities in host cities – are discussed.*

Lenskyj, Helen Jefferson. *Gender Politics and the Olympic Industry*. Basingstoke: Palgrave Macmillan, 2013.
DOI: 10.1057/9781137291158.

DOI: 10.1057/9781137291158

The preceding discussion has addressed a range of issues relating to gender, sex and sexualities, in the broader context of interlocking systems of oppression. Taking a critical sociological approach, the analysis has focused on historical and contemporary constructions of and challenges to hegemonic femininities and masculinities in the context of Olympic sport. In this chapter, I continue to examine these themes, with a particular focus on sex, and the ways in which it implicitly or explicitly shapes debates about performance-enhancing drugs, the exploitation of athletes' bodies in advertising and the IOC's gender verification process, with special attention to the case of Caster Semenya.

Issues relating to sex and sexualities are played out not only on the sports fields but also in boardrooms and on the streets. Behind the scenes of the multifaceted Olympic industry, problems range from sexual harassment perpetrated by male IOC members to "street sweeps" targeting sex trade workers and sexual minorities in host cities and regions. In these seemingly disparate examples, a common theme is the sexual vulnerability of women and disadvantaged minorities in the face of powerful Olympic industry and state officials. Following a discussion of these issues, I conclude the chapter by contrasting feminists' differing priorities before and during the 2010 Vancouver Olympics. While sport feminists' efforts were directed at convincing the IOC to include women's ski jump in the 2010 Winter Olympics programme, feminist community workers focused their attention on protecting homeless women and sex trade workers from the violence and exploitation associated with sporting mega-events.

Femininity first

From the early years of girls' and women's sporting participation in western countries, the spectre of a "loss of femininity" loomed large in the minds of medical experts, educators and other guardians of female morality. Underlying the stated concerns about physical appearance – sweat, muscles, short hair and flat chests that allegedly rendered sportswomen unattractive to men – were the barely concealed issues of sex, sexual identity and reproductive capacity. The terminology used to refer to sex was, of course, historically and culturally specific. In the years when Victorian attitudes continued to hold sway, sex and sexuality were rarely named explicitly, and public discourse on sex/sport issues was cloaked in euphemistic and medical language.

DOI: 10.1057/9781137291158

As developments in the field of sexology, most notably the work of Krafft-Ebing and Freud, became more widely known in the first three decades of the 20th century, women whose appearance and comportment appeared non-conforming attracted more negative attention. Labels such as "mannish" and "Amazonian," used in earlier times as descriptors, became code words for "lesbian." By the 1960s, even the relatively benign term "tomboy" had been pathologized as sexologists added it to the set of behaviours associated with "childhood gender nonconformity" and lesbianism.[1]

A list of sport-related reproductive problems, first developed in the early 1900s and expanded over the century, included "dropped uterus," infertility, loss of virginity, over-developed pelvic muscles, delayed menarche and secondary amenorrhoea (temporary cessation of menstruation). (Delayed menarche and temporary menstrual irregularities were the only issues that were supported by later research evidence, with low body fat and strenuous training shown to be key contributing factors, and the related problem of low bone density in female athletes remains a health concern.)

Prohibitions against vigorous exercise, or any exercise, during menstruation had a long history, but the availability of the tampon in western countries in the 1940s and 1950s proved a liberating factor for later generations of sportswomen.[2] However, even in 1958, the British Medical Association advised women who were menstruating "not to swim in any enclosed pools or doubtful water, to keep out of heavy surf, and not to dive deeply."[3] Regardless of the warnings and restrictions, the women who competed in international competition presumably found ways of dealing with these issues. Furthermore, in view of the incidence of secondary amenorrhea among sportswomen, it is possible that managing menstruation was not a recurring problem for some.

The "sexual revolution" of the 1950s and 1960s in western countries, aided by advances in contraception for women, broke the silence on some sex-related issues, while the "gay revolution" focused public, media and scientific attention squarely on sex and sexuality. On the issue of sexual identity, the (faulty) logic of the 1950s took this format: sport attracts lesbians; therefore sport creates lesbians. There may have been a grain of truth in the "sport attracts lesbians" theory, because in Canada, the US and elsewhere, community-based recreational sports, especially softball, offered a relatively safe place for women of all sexual orientations to play and to socialize. By the 1960s, homophobia was taking a

DOI: 10.1057/9781137291158

new, more sinister form: the allegation that lesbians in sport recruited straight women.[4] One result was the ongoing stigmatization of women, particularly "unfeminine" women, who played team sports or sports considered the rightful domain of men.

Sex tests: checking for "real women"

Confusion between sexual orientation, sex-role orientation and gender-role non-conformity led to suspicions that women who "didn't look like real women" might be men. All this provided fertile ground for the IOC to introduce sex testing, a practice that sociologist Jaime Schultz aptly labelled "disciplining sex."[5] Developments in the sex test from 1966 to 1998 – from "nude parade" to so-called scientific evidence – have been extensively documented and critiqued.[6]

In 1966, the IAAF practice was to have female gynaecologists look at the nude women, back and front, and there are anecdotal reports of female coaches who conducted the same kind of visual inspection in the 1960s. A 2009 account of Caster Semenya's earlier experiences stated that she was subjected to this kind of humiliation as a high school athlete in the first decade of the 21st century. The test soon evolved into an internal pelvic exam ("searching for hidden testes"), and, in 1968, a lab test of cheek cells (buccal smear test) to assess chromosomes.[7] The science of the day was incomplete and flawed; for example, it had not been proven that an extra Y chromosome gave women any sporting advantage.

Australian sprinter Raelene Boyle described her experience of the sex test in 1968, when Olympic candidates were subjected to an eight-hour ordeal, carried out in a university's veterinary clinic, in order to establish that they were female. In addition to requiring the young women to share intimate information verbally and in writing, the test involved a visual inspection of their genitals by male doctors. As Boyle reported, "It was frightfully disconcerting, at 16, to walk into a room with a much older guy and be told: 'Pull your pants down.'"[8]

To subject only women to the test gave the clear message that their athletic performances would always be inferior to men's, and so the gender of female athletes in international competition needed to be confirmed in order to rule out the possibility of male impostors. To date, there is only one proven case of a man taking part in a women's Olympic event.

DOI: 10.1057/9781137291158

German athlete Heinrich Ratjen competed as a woman, reportedly on Hitler's orders; he came fourth in the women's high jump at the 1936 Olympics.

Over the years, sex tests prompted extensive protest from doctors, female athletes and their allies because of their invasiveness as well as their inaccuracy. The IOC finally suspended testing in 2000, but neither the IOC nor the international federations ceased their scrutiny of athletes who were "not woman enough," with special attention paid to those who won world championships or Olympic medals. Caster Semenya became the foremost example of yet another victim of abusive treatment at the hands of the IAAF and the IOC.

It is interesting to speculate on how outcomes might have differed if performance-enhancing drugs had not been anabolic steroids, which produce visible virilizing effects on female athletes. Not coincidentally, the IOC introduced both sex testing and drug testing in the same year, 1967. When men have uncommon "genetic gifts" (in reality, genetic abnormalities) that predispose them towards success in a specific sport, they are called sporting heroes. For women, these "gifts" are liabilities that open the door to invasive testing regimes, public humiliation and finally, in some cases, the stripping of their records and medals.

Discussing Semenya, physiologist Tim Oakes asked, "What do we call a male who has a biological advantage? We call him Usain Bolt."[9] Other critics argued that most high performance athletes, almost by definition, have some form of genetic advantage.[10] But for Semenya, at 19 years of age, having a biological advantage could well become a tragedy. Although she made dramatic but not unprecedented improvements in the 800 metre race in 2009, her performance did not come close to the world record or even the top 10 fastest times.[11] It appears that she was subjected to such a high level of scrutiny because, in the view of critics, she was too muscular and had a deep voice, facial hair, narrow hips and "masculine" features. But as Leonard Cheune, head of South African athletes, asked, "Who are white people to question the makeup of an African girl? ... It is outrageous for people from other countries to tell us 'We want to take her to a laboratory because we don't like her nose, or her figure.' I say this is racism, pure and simple."[12]

Black South Africans and others drew parallels with the early 19th-century public degradation of the African woman Saartjie Baartman, a 19-year-old slave whom European scientists exhibited as a "sexual freak"

DOI: 10.1057/9781137291158

in Europe and England.[13] There was widespread support in Semenya's rural community and beyond, as well as censure for "the intolerance and prurience of western commentators."[14] An Australian newspaper, *The Age*, had the dubious distinction of being among the first to announce that Semenya had both male and female sexual organs, was "technically a hermaphrodite" (an outdated term for intersexed) and had three times the testosterone of a "normal female."[15] One can only imagine the stresses of the lengthy procedures that generated this result. Semenya was examined by an endocrinologist, a psychologist, a gynaecologist, an internal medicine specialist and a "gender expert" and subjected to numerous blood tests and chromosome tests, and then, in the ultimate invasion of her privacy, the results were spread around the world.

After six months' deliberation, the IAAF announced that medical experts would now allow Semenya to compete, following unspecified medical interventions that had taken place in the interim. The IOC and the IAAF used the occasion to develop a set of guidelines to deal with future cases of so-called sexual-development disorders (SDSs), specifically intersexuality, which was formulated as a health problem in need of correction before the athlete would be readmitted to Olympic competition. Incredibly, the impetus for any initial screening – the first step that would then lead to a battery of tests, and ultimately to hormone therapy and surgery – required "sport authorities to send *photographs* of the women suspected of having SDS" (emphasis added). As Judith Butler noted, the Semenya investigation procedure revealed that "sex determination is decided by consensus," and asked, "is this not a presumption that sex is a social negotiation of some kind?"[16] In other words, sex determination is shaped by social and cultural assumptions about femaleness and maleness. This, of course, is not news, but for it to be formalized and applied globally in this way is an extremely disturbing development.

With the IOC and IAAF procedures now in place, the stage is set for yet more instances of racist treatment of a Black female athlete – and, indeed, discriminatory treatment of *any* female athlete – whenever sport authorities act upon a fixed idea of what gender-appropriate behaviour, appearance and comportment should *look* like. As Schultz aptly pointed out, a purported technology of sex was actually a technology of gender.[17] Except for invoking 21st-century medical science (which, in the areas of sex, intersex, genetics and related issues, remains imprecise), the attitudes reflected in the official guidelines could have come from the 1928

DOI: 10.1057/9781137291158

"experts" who looked at a group of nine tired women and pronounced that the 800 metre race was beyond women's capacity.

It is equally shocking to witness the power of the IOC and the IAAF to force a young woman to undergo hormone therapy, even surgery, not in the interests of her health, but simply to satisfy their largely arbitrary definition of "woman." In this scenario, hormonal manipulation, prohibited in world sport, is permissible when it is controlled by Olympic industry officials. The policy brings to mind the brutal medical practices of the last century aimed at "normalizing" non-conforming women (especially those considered to have too much, or not enough, interest in heterosexual sex) through enforced "rest cures," hysterectomies or electroshock treatments.

The IOC eliminated sex tests for the 2000 Sydney Olympics, and its ruling on the eligibility of transsexual athletes took effect for the 2004 Athens Games. Organizers of the Gay Games and OutGames adopted the same policy as the IOC for their future events. Interestingly, while there had been decades of protest against the discriminatory, stigmatizing and potentially inaccurate sex tests, lobbying for the rights of transsexual sportspeople had a relatively short history. Predictably, the IOC's eligibility policy for transsexual athletes was based on conservative, medicalized criteria, and, as sociologist Heather Sykes pointed out in 2006, it "continues to exclude many transgender and intersex competitors."[18] Clearly, the situation that confronted Semenya a few years later confirmed her analysis. Ironically, as one feminist commentator pointed out, the new transsexual policy would, in theory, enable Semenya to compete as a man if she chose transgender surgery,[19] whereas there was no clear policy enabling her to establish her right to compete as a woman.

In many western countries, individuals have the right to choose whether they want to live as a woman or as a man. Regardless of anatomy and physiology, gender is fundamentally a matter of self-definition – but not if that person is an athlete. Despite scientific recognition of naturally occurring genetic variations among humans, as well as evidence showing that such variations in women do not necessarily give them an advantage, world sport remains one of the slowest social institutions to adopt more fluid definitions of gender. After more than a century of preoccupation with sex binaries and discomfort with sexual and gender ambiguity, the IOC and the IAAF continue their rigorous policing of sex and gender, purportedly in the interests of fairness in competition.

DOI: 10.1057/9781137291158

Sex, drugs and anti-drug campaigns

Sex and sex binaries were at the core of several American anti-drug campaigns in the 1980s, including those conducted on college and university campuses. A 1992 media analysis of visual images and texts conducted by Laurel Davis and Linda Delano showed a clear pattern of physical gender dichotomization: the predominant message that anyone who took steroids, or whose body fell outside the categories of male and female for any other reason, was "freakish," "abnormal and disgusting" and "not fully human."[20]

Expanding on Davis and Delano's analysis, I noted the emergence of a consistent pattern in these texts and images: greater emphasis on the threat to gender boundaries than on the significant health risks, including sterility, heart disease and cancer. Since the word "steroids" was closely associated in the public mind with the so-called male hormone testosterone (although it is present in small amounts in women as well as men), the emphasis on sex was no doubt considered a sure means of attracting young people's attention.

Most posters targeted men, with a focus on the sexually charged issues of enlarged breasts and atrophied genitals. One poster stated, "It's a myth that all the really big jocks take steroids" and showed a jockstrap labelled "SMALL," with a tiny pouch. Another, with a photo of a person's chest area and small breasts, carried the caption "The obscene thing is, this is a man." In short, drugs threaten the "super-stud" reputation of male athletes, and images of women's bare breasts are obscene.

A poster directed at women conveyed a range of messages about what it meant to be a "feminine" athlete. The photo showed a woman with the kind of upper-body muscular development that would be expected in an athlete, but with a noticeable bulge in her pubic area. The text read:

> Steroids: They'll make a man out of you yet. Women who take steroids begin to lose their feminine characteristics. Unless you consider a lowered voice, baldness, facial hair, shrunken breasts and uncontrollable aggression feminine.[21]

Unsurprisingly, femininity was defined largely by appearance, with any variations in voice, facial hair and breast size in effect pathologized. The side effect of aggression was not mentioned in texts targeting men, presumably because it is considered an asset in male athletes, but "unnatural" in women. The body type and facial features of the woman

DOI: 10.1057/9781137291158

in the photo suggested an Eastern European track and field athlete, and therefore, it was implied, not someone whom young American sports-women would, or should, wish to emulate.

A girl problem: puberty

A different kind of drug problem involving girls and women was hinted at in the 1970s, but has received less public and scientific attention. Russian Olga Korbut and Romanian Nadia Comaneci, the two gymnasts who received "perfect tens" in the 1972 and 1976 Olympics, not only pioneered a new level of athleticism in women's gymnastics but also confronted audiences with a new concept of the female gymnast's body. Comparisons have often been made with Russian Ludmilla Tourischeva, a champion gymnast in the 1960s; at 20 years of age in 1972, she had the secondary sex characteristics – specifically, breasts and hips – of a fully matured young woman. Korbut, at age 17, and Comaneci, 15, had the bodies of lean, muscular, prepubescent girls, leading to rumours that they had been given puberty-delaying drugs. Similar concerns surfaced during the 2008 Beijing Olympics in relation to Chinese female gym-nasts. In addition to allegations that some of them were under the age of 16, the possibility of puberty-delaying drugs was also raised, significantly, after the American team lost to China.

Following allegations from the coaches of the American team, Béla and Márta Károlyi, the Chinese coach was quoted as saying, "If you think our girls are little because of looks, then maybe you should think the Europeans and Americans are strong because of doping."[22] This exchange brings to mind the controversy over Caster Semenya, and the South African official's comment concerning non-Africans' judgement of an African woman's body. In the case of the Chinese gymnasts, other obvious factors included the fact that Chinese people as an ethnic group are small, and the self-selecting process in the sport, with smaller female bodies being better suited to the gymnastics routines that have been developed over the past three decades.

Again, such rumours are more likely to take root in western countries when the alleged perpetrators are the "other," in this case, Chinese or Eastern European coaches and sports medicine personnel. Yet coaches from western countries often point to the "problem" of girls reach-ing puberty and carefully monitor the weight of female gymnasts, in particular, to delay menarche. (The combination of low body fat and a demanding training programme delays the process to some extent.) In

DOI: 10.1057/9781137291158

1997, a Canadian figure skating technical coordinator identified puberty as a problem, saying, "until they [girls] finish puberty, you never know what the final *product* is going to be" (emphasis added). As the article explained, "growth throws off the timing of jumps, widening hips put the brakes on tight rotations in jumps."[23]

Presumably some of these issues are addressed by age categories. Different judging criteria, reflecting the strengths and the limitations of prepubescent and post-pubescent females, would also help to alleviate the perceived problem. However, as in gymnastics, debates over athleticism versus artistry continue to influence judging and performance, with ever-escalating expectations placed on female skaters to master moves such as triple jumps that were formerly included only in men's routines. The related issue of the increasingly young age of competitive skaters, gymnasts and swimmers is also problematic, since it raises an additional set of ethical issues for the adults involved, especially in residential sport institutes where staff members are *in loco parentis*.

The IOC: behind the scenes

Although the inner workings of the IOC, often characterized as a private men's club, are largely kept concealed, there is ample evidence that gender politics are at work behind the scenes as well as in the more public aspects of the Olympic industry. For a start, the IOC did not invite women to become members until 1981, and 30 years later the number had crept up only to 19 (17 per cent). At that rate it will take almost 60 years before it reaches 50 per cent. (I am not suggesting that gender parity is a worthwhile target since, as I explained at the outset, such reforms will not address the fundamental flaws in the Olympic industry.)

During the 1998–9 exposés of the bribery and corruption involving IOC members and bid committees, the first IOC member to resign was one of the two original female members, Pirjo Haeggman of Finland. Two months after resigning, perhaps having noticed that some of her male counterparts with more damning evidence against them had avoided expulsion, she unsuccessfully requested the IOC to reinstate her. It is significant, too, that the Black and ethnic minority men found to have been involved in the scandals were more likely to be expelled than the white men, most of whom received only warnings.[24]

A less publicized feature of the bribery scandal was the sexual behaviour of some male IOC members during host city visits, and, conversely, the sexual enticements offered by some bid committees, all of which gave

DOI: 10.1057/9781137291158

a new meaning to the truism "sex sells sport." In the period before the so-called reforms, every IOC member, usually accompanied by family members, received grand tours of all bid cities, where host committees welcomed them as VIPs. Some assumed that their privileges included the sexual services of any woman associated with the bid committee, and in some instances, they were correct. As early as 1958, when IOC members were visiting Tokyo during the bid process for the 1964 Olympics, the Tokyo bid committee allocated each member a female companion, as well as providing professional prostitutes in the hotel reserved for the IOC visitors.[25]

Investigative journalist Andrew Jennings labelled one IOC member "Mr. Wandering Hands." While doing research in the archives of Falun, a Swedish city that had submitted unsuccessful bids for several Winter Olympics, Jennings found clear evidence of sexual harassment: letters from IOC members marked "private and confidential" that covered up a "sex scandal." As he explained, Swedish politicians, sports leaders and businessmen believed that winning the Games "was more important than protecting innocent women from being abused by dirty old men…there's a number of male IOC members who know it's safe to abuse and harass those pretty young women employed as hostesses by every city bidding for the Olympics."[26] That these same men wield power in the organization that defines itself as "the moral authority for world sport" and support its mission statement, which identifies "women's participation in sporting activities and the Olympic Games" as one of its major concerns,[27] speaks volumes about their hypocrisy.

A more recent example of hypocrisy involved FIFA president Sepp Blatter, who is also an IOC member, speaking on the topic of the 2022 World Cup host, Qatar. When asked whether gays and lesbians attending the event should be concerned because of the illegality of homosexuality in that country, he assured them that there would be no problem "because football…does not affect [sic] any discrimination." But he advised, "They should refrain from any sexual activity."[28] After the widespread outcry that followed, he issued the standard (reverse) apology, regretting "if somebody feels hurt."[29]

It is quite possible that the IOC will one day follow FIFA's lead in awarding a future Olympics to Qatar or another city in the Arabian peninsula, recognizing that the region offers "a non-exploited terrain for investment." As sociologists Mahfoud Amara and Eleni Theodoraki explain, international sports organizations "are continuing in their

DOI: 10.1057/9781137291158

business oriented efforts of diffusing their products (i.e. sports as commodities and spectacles) worldwide and maintaining their dominance over global (business) sporting affairs."[30] There are obvious implications for women and sexual minorities, either as participants or as spectators, which have yet to be investigated.

Sweep the streets, the Olympics are coming

The suppression of protest and the "sanitizing" of the Olympic host city are phenomena that have a long and disturbing history, beginning with the Berlin Olympics of 1936 and continuing unabated into the 21st century. The most common human targets have been homeless people, Romanis, sex trade workers, activists, protesters, gays and lesbians, and the most frequent geographic targets have been innercity and working-class neighbourhoods. In many instances, police and private security forces, empowered by short- and long-term legislation criminalizing poverty and homelessness, have forcibly removed men, women and children from the streets or from squats, as well as arresting protesters. In relation to the forced removal of homeless people from the streets, there are clear gender-related implications, since women are vulnerable to sexual assaults in addition to the dangers that face both men and women who live on the streets. Furthermore, escalating rents and evictions without cause in innercity neighbourhoods – the results of Olympic-driven urban profiteering – increase the numbers of homeless people in host cities.

Pre-Olympic street sweeps have not been confined to totalitarian regimes; they have been carried out in most host countries for decades. While these trends have been well documented,[31] underlying issues related to sex and sexualities merit further investigation. The 1936 Berlin pre-Games cleanup, a propaganda move following Nazi officials' promises to the US Olympic Committee, included the temporary removal of anti-Jewish signs from the streets and the censoring of the most extreme racism in the Nazi press. In addition, in a move to reassure foreign visitors, Germany suspended its anti-homosexual laws for three weeks.[32]

In subsequent cleanups in host cities, gays and lesbians, as well as sex trade workers and homeless people, were more likely to be targeted than protected. The goal was "imagineering" (image-making and/through social engineering), as American sociologist Charles Rutheiser

DOI: 10.1057/9781137291158

termed it in his critical analysis of Atlanta's preparations for the 1996 Olympics.[33] More is at stake than creating a short-term image of a "clean" city. According to Olympic industry rhetoric, hosting the Games produces "world class city status," thereby attracting multinational investment and boosting tourism. The presence of "undesirables," however defined, detracts from the image, serving as a visible reminder of social inequalities.

Gay sex = vice

The criminalizing of gay sexual activities in Canada in the period before the 1976 Montreal Olympics not only reflected the official labelling of gay sex, like prostitution, as "vice," but also suggested a kind of puritanical embarrassment at the prospect that Olympic visitors might actually see gay men and lesbians on the streets. In 1975, the Royal Canadian Mounted Police (RCMP) started a campaign of political repression that led to the naming of activists, especially gay and lesbian activists, as "security threats." In their comprehensive analysis of the *Canadian War on Queers*, sociologists Gary Kinsman and Patrizia Gentile called these processes "moral cleansing" and "sexual policing."[34] These events amply demonstrate the zeal with which police and politicians have colluded with Olympic industry officials in their campaigns to clean up the image of the host city and country.

Although most Olympic events in 1976 were held in Montreal, Quebec, some were located in other cities in Quebec and Ontario, giving the police an excuse to expand their campaign over two provinces. At that time in Canada, consensual sex between men or between women had been decriminalized, but, when they deemed it necessary, police used a 1917 "bawdy-house" law in order to define gay sex acts as "acts of indecency." The upcoming Olympics provided one such occasion, and the RCMP and local police began a series of raids on gay and lesbian bars and clubs and gay bathhouses. Intimidation was an obvious motive. On some occasions, they carried submachine guns and broke down doors with axes. As well as photographing and arresting patrons, they seized membership lists, alleging that gay baths were fronts for prostitution. In Montreal, this police campaign quickly led to the formation of a new organization, Comité Homosexuel Anti-Répression/Gay Coalition against Repression (CHAR), and English- and French-speaking activists

DOI: 10.1057/9781137291158

together carried out a number of gay rights demonstrations, the largest held up to that time, prompting solidarity demonstrations in other Canadian cities as well.

Gays and lesbians were not the only victims; police also targeted leftist groups suspected of planning protests during the Olympics, and some activists were warned to leave town during the Games. People arrested for homelessness or drunkenness could expect a long sentence aimed at keeping them off the streets for the duration – up to six months instead of a few days.[35]

A directive from the Montreal organizing committee (COJO) was quite explicit concerning gays and lesbians. In an area from Quebec City to Toronto, "all non-conforming elements of which homosexuals are included, must be *confined and made hidden*" (emphasis added).[36] Stuart Russell, a member CHAR's coordinating committee and a leader of the Young Socialists, was employed as a telex operator with COJO. Shortly after he participated in a CHAR protest march past the COJO offices, he was fired on the grounds that he was a "security risk" (that is, gay). This was the fourth time that COJO had fired workers for political reasons within a few months, and CHAR demanded Russell's reinstatement as well as full disclosure of the grounds for his dismissal. Messages of solidarity came from gay liberation groups in New York, London, Scotland, Northern Ireland, Denmark and Australia. The Montreal Citizens' Movement supported CHAR, and the Quebec Civil Liberties Union lodged a complaint with the Quebec Human Rights Commission, claiming that COJO had discriminated against the four employees on the basis of political convictions. They were denied access to RCMP documents on the grounds of "national security," and so the human rights complaints could not proceed.[37] Like many arms of the Olympic industry, the Montreal organizing committee and the Canadian police collaborated to ensure that the Olympic rings remained untarnished.[38]

Sex trade workers at risk

Cleanup initiatives aimed at sex trade workers in Olympic host cities have a long history, with the legal status of prostitution in host countries a key factor in shaping outcomes. Before the 1992 Barcelona Olympics, for example, police crackdowns targeted prostitutes, transvestites, homeless people and dissidents.[39] Events in Seoul in the years before the

DOI: 10.1057/9781137291158

1988 Olympics took a different turn, with the so-called beautification programme resulting in more than one million forced "relocations," on the one hand, while the government used the "shameless" promotion of sex tourism to market South Korea.[40]

Since the 2004 Athens Olympics and the 2006 World Cup in Germany, links between sport mega-events, prostitution and sex trafficking (human trafficking for the purpose of prostitution) have attracted the attention of governments and sex worker advocacy and protection groups, as well as researchers. The influx of tourists increases demand, and traffickers see heightened business opportunities in Olympic host cities. In addition, international sporting events facilitate the entry of trafficked victims in the guise of "visitors." As the head of a Greek NGO that supported victims explained, "Pushed by poverty, pulled by hopeful dreams of life in the West, and exploited by opportunists, women suspend disbelief and their better judgment and gamble on a better life."[41]

Greece did not pass an anti-trafficking law until 2002, and was a transit and destination country for the trafficking of women and children (particularly Romani children) from Eastern Europe. In 2004, the government took steps to support victims and NGOs, and to increase enforcement efforts (for the first time punishing police who were complicit with traffickers). Despite these efforts, Greek government figures showed a 95 per cent increase in victims identified by authorities between 2003 and 2004, followed by a decline of 24 per cent the following year, for the most part a reflection of the country's status as Olympic host.[42]

Brothels had been legalized in 1999, but in 2003 city officials in Athens tried to close down 15 brothels for violating the law limiting brothel employees to three. Media reports mistakenly claimed that this was an attempt to increase the number of brothels (not an illogical conclusion), and this prompted charges of sex tourism. In a counterstrike, the Greek sex workers' union pointed out that the authorities failed to enforce the law against unregistered sex workers, while unfairly targeting those who were registered.[43]

In countries where prostitution was illegal, the upcoming hosting of the Olympics prompted governments to consider legalization, thereby reopening debates about the risks and benefits of doing so, with religious organizations, advocacy groups, politicians and police unlikely to find common ground. In some host cities, the legalization controversy attracted more media and public attention than activists' efforts to stop human trafficking and to strengthen existing policies. Female prostitutes'

DOI: 10.1057/9781137291158

groups and feminist advocacy groups often took opposing sides in the debates, the former citing the (relative) safety of legalized brothels, while the latter focused on the underlying causes of poverty, addictions and child sexual abuse, making the point that no child says she wants to be a sex trade worker when she grows up.

Advocacy efforts have had limited success. Before the Vancouver 2010 Olympics, the Citizens Summit, a coalition of women's groups, academics and politicians, gave the organizing committee and the provincial and federal governments a grade of F for "failing to make sure women and youth are secure against human trafficking during the 2010 Olympics."[44]

In the lead-up to the London 2012 Olympics, women's groups worked to raise awareness of sex trafficking and to prevent harassment and violence against women, all problems exacerbated by sport mega-events. The London organizing committee and local governments responded by circulating information on sex trafficking and sexual harassment and assault laws to relevant groups. A flyer distributed by End Violence Against Women pointed out that "for women the Games are more likely to be a threat to their safety than terrorism." According to the text,

> Construction workers have been found soliciting prostitution during police kerb-crawling operations in the Olympics host boroughs, while the already limited support services for women in prostitution are facing a funding crisis … The Games are bringing a huge influx of people to Britain: 100,000 workers; more than 10,000 athletes; 20,000 media representatives.[45]

The emphasis on "visitors, workers and athletes," as well as the singling out of construction workers, carried with it an underlying and perhaps unintentional message that it was these "other" men, non-British and/or working-class, who lacked understanding of British law and were likely to be involved in sex trafficking or coercive sex.

Ski jumpers and sex workers: poles apart?

The campaign asking the IOC to include women's ski jump in the Vancouver 2010 Olympics started in 2006 with a human rights complaint and culminated in a 2009 court decision, during which period this remained a high priority among liberal sport feminists in Canada and elsewhere. After failing in their lobbying efforts directed at the Vancouver Organizing Committee for the Olympic Games (VANOC)

DOI: 10.1057/9781137291158

and the IOC, the ski jumpers, with support from sport feminist groups, eventually filed a lawsuit against VANOC.

Details of the arguments, court hearings and appeal process attracted the attention of feminist scholars as well as activists, with extensive analyses of the final, unsuccessful outcome filling the pages of law journals and feminist publications.[46] To summarize, the case, involving more than 160 female ski jumpers from 18 countries, rested on the complaint that the inclusion of the men's event and the exclusion of the women's violated the Canadian Charter of Rights and Freedoms, and that, since the 2010 Olympics would be conducted on Canadian soil, the organizers were bound by the sex equality provisions of the Charter. As I observed at the time, it seemed naïve to assume that the IOC, the "moral authority on world sport," would consider itself to be subject to the laws of any host country. Nevertheless, the case proceeded to the Supreme Court of British Columbia and then to the British Columbia Supreme Court of Appeal. As a non-lawyer, I read the rather confusing decision to mean the following: yes, VANOC was a governmental institution, and, yes, it was also a non-governmental institution; therefore, yes, it was subject to the Charter provisions and no, it wasn't. As one commentary noted, the IOC simply got VANOC to do its "sexist 'dirty work.'"[47]

In a rare critical analysis of the case (that is, critical of the case, not just the ruling), sociologist Ann Travers identified the "deafening silence of sex segregation, whiteness and wealth" evident in the assumptions about Canadian women, citizenship and democracy embedded in discourse surrounding the case.[48] Plaintiffs acknowledged that VANOC was not the decision-maker in the process, but suggested that the court could force VANOC to take a stand vis-à-vis the IOC, by saying that it could not legally stage a men's event without a women's event. If the female ski jumpers had expected solidarity from their male counterparts, they were sadly mistaken. As Travers reported, the counsel for the defence reacted with shock at the "unthinkability" of dropping the men's event. She noted, "After all, it is one thing to extend, to include; it is another to share resources through redistribution."[49] Furthermore, the opportunities for displays of Canadian nationalism would be jeopardized if a controversial court ruling interfered with the men's event and left Canada in an embarrassing situation in the eyes of the world. Yet, as noted earlier, there are some precedents for this kind of solidarity on the part of men in sport administration, such as the position taken in 1929 by the American Athletic Union, which threatened to withdraw all male athletes from the

DOI: 10.1057/9781137291158

1932 Olympics if women were not allowed to compete in track and field events.

Questions of class and race privilege were invisible in the proceedings, and, with the exception of Travers' article, in most subsequent analyses. Access to training in snow sports is constrained by socioeconomic status, and ski jump facilities, in particular, are expensive to build and maintain. In Canada, they are rarely found outside ski resorts that have hosted past Winter Olympics. Furthermore, the "new racism," as anti-racist scholars have termed it, relies on "colourblindness."[50] In other words, failure even to talk about the whiteness of athletes in Winter Olympic sports resulted in "(at best) an unthinking complicity" supporting classism and racism on the part of all the individuals and institutions involved.[51]

Travers' claims take on particular relevance when one considers the life-and-death situations that a different group of Canadian women faced – homeless women living in the Downtown Eastside (DTES) of Vancouver. During the same period that the ski jump case was before the Human Rights Commission and the Vancouver courts, there was another high-profile case involving women. A trial that began in 2006 and continued until 2010 involved a British Columbia man charged with murdering dozens of women who had disappeared from the Vancouver area since 1999. He was eventually found guilty of six of the murders. The trial drew public attention to the hundreds of missing women in the province, particularly those who had last been seen in northern British Columbia between Prince George and Prince Rupert on a stretch of highway now known as the Highway of Tears. Many of these young women, including a disproportionate number of Native women, came from the DTES, and Native activists and feminist groups accused police of failing to investigate these disappearances for years. As one Native woman summed up their attitude, her daughter was "just another dead Indian."[52]

The DTES, the poorest urban postal code in Canada, has very serious problems related to homelessness, violence, drugs and prostitution, and about 30 per cent of the homeless people are Native. Equally significant is the fact that the availability of cheap accommodation in single-room-occupancy hotels plummeted as a result of the Vancouver 2010 Olympics, thereby adding to the numbers of homeless people,[53] as well as the potential for human trafficking and violence when women lived on the streets. In this context, with the Olympics imminent, a top priority for the feminists who worked in the DTES was the safety of homeless women and Native women.

DOI: 10.1057/9781137291158

Many of the activists involved in the Olympic Resistance Network (ORN) were frontline workers in the DTES. Harsha Walia, for example, was active in the Downtown Eastside Women's Centre. Established in 1978, the centre provided a safe place and practical support for women and children who were vulnerable to exploitation and violence, and offered education, advocacy and peer mentorship.[54] In her contribution to a roundtable published in 2009, Walia discussed the Olympic resistance campaigns and the concept of convergence. As she explained, groups involved in the ORN included Native communities that opposed the expansion of ski resorts in the mountains; a coalition of middle-class residents, Native people and environmentalists that fought against destruction of a forested area at Eagle Ridge Bluffs; the anti-poverty struggles in the DTES; "a migrant justice movement led by immigrant/racialized people, and a vibrant anti-imperialist movement involving many in exile."[55] ORN's rallying cry, "No Olympics on Stolen Land," was a reference to the fact that Indigenous lands in British Columbia had not been the subject of a treaty. In short, these convergence initiatives represented intersectionality in action.

I have juxtaposed the ski jump case and the DTES women's plight to illustrate the markedly different priorities of two different groups of Canadian feminist activists at the time of the Vancouver 2010 Olympics: liberal feminists focusing on equal Olympic opportunity, on the one hand, and radical and socialist feminists protecting homeless and Native women, on the other. It would be naïve to suggest that the former group should have been out on the DTES streets, but I do question whether the fund-raising efforts that went towards the "court costs and travel expenses"[56] associated with the ski jump case might have been better spent on "bread" not "circuses."

Conclusion

This discussion has tackled a range of sex-related issues in order to demonstrate that questions of gender, sex and sexualities, further complicated by differences in social class and ethnicity, permeate every aspect of the Olympic industry. As anti-racist feminists have emphasized, efforts to end discrimination are futile if they target only one of the many interlocking systems of oppression that serve the interests of the dominant group.

DOI: 10.1057/9781137291158

Notes

1   M. Saghir and E. Robbins, *Male and Female Homosexuality* (Baltimore, MD: Williams & Wilkins, 1973).

2   H. Lenskyj, *Out of Bounds: Women, Sport and Sexuality* (Toronto: Women's Press, 1986).

3   Cited in M. Stell, *Half the Race: A History of Australian Women in Sport* (Sydney: Angus & Robertson, 1991), 179.

4   See S. Cahn, *Coming on Strong: Gender and Sexuality in Twentieth-Century Women's Sport* (Cambridge, MA: Harvard University Press, 1994); P. Griffin, *Strong Women, Deep Closets* (Champaign, IL: Human Kinetics, 1998); M. A. Hall, *The Girl and the Game* (Toronto: University of Toronto Press, 2002); Lenskyj, *Out of Bounds*.

5   J. Schultz, Disciplining Sex: "Gender Verification" Policies and Women's Sport, in H. Lenskyj and S. Wagg (eds), *Handbook of Olympic Studies* (Basingstoke, UK: Palgrave Macmillan, 2012), 443–60.

6   See, for example, A. Fausto-Sterling, *Sexing the Body* (New York: Basic Books, 2000), chapter 1; Schultz; A. Schweinbenz and A. Cronk, Femininity Control at the Olympic Games, *Third Space* 9:2 (2010), http://www.thirdspace.ca/journal/article/view/schweinbenzcronk

7   Caster Semenya, *New York Times* (August 26, 2009), http://topics.nytimes.com/topics/reference/timestopics/people/s/caster_semenya/index.html

8   Raelene Boyle quoted in Stell, 177.

9   Dr. Tim Noakes quoted on M. Ginnane (dir.), *Too Fast To Be a Woman*, *The Passionate Eye* (Ottawa: CBC Television, August 31, 2011).

10   M. Merck, The Question of Caster Semenya, *Radical Philosophy* 180 (March/April 2010), 6.

11   Schultz, 453.

12   D. Smith, Caster Semenya Row: "Who Are White People to Question the Makeup of an African Girl? It Is Racism," *The Observer* (August 23, 2009), http://www.guardian.co.uk/sport/2009/aug/23/caster-semenya-athletics-gender

13   C. McGreal, Coming Home, *The Guardian* (February 21, 2002), http://www.guardian.co.uk/education/2002/feb/21/internationaleducationnews.highereducation; Caster Semenya, *New York Times*.

14   Smith, Caster Semenya Row.

15   World Champ Semenya's Gender Mystery Solved, *The Age* (September 11, 2009), http://www.theage.com.au/world/world-champ-semenyas-gender-mystery-solved-20090911-fjjq.html

16   Butler quoted in Merck, 4.

17   Schultz, 452.

18   H. Sykes, Transsexual and Transgender Policies in Sport, *Women in Sport and Physical Activity Journal* 15:1 (2006), 3–12. The complex topic of transsexual

DOI: 10.1057/9781137291158

athletes is beyond the scope of this discussion, and has been examined in depth
by many other scholars. In short, the policy change came into effect for the
2004 Athens Olympics and permitted trans people to compete under certain
conditions: the athlete's gender is legally recognized; the athlete has completed
genital reconstructive surgery and had his or her ovaries or testes removed;
the athlete has undergone a minimum of two years' post-operative hormone
therapy to eliminate any sex-related advantages. See S. Teetzel, Equality, Equity,
and Inclusion: Issues in Women and Transgendered Athletes' Participation
at the Olympics, in N. Crowther, R. Barney, and M. Heine (eds), *Cultural
Imperialism in Action*, Proceedings of the Eighth International Symposium
for Olympic Research (London, ON: University of Western Ontario, 2006),
331–8; H. S. Cavanagh and H. Sykes, Transsexual Bodies at the Olympics: The
International Olympic Committee's Policy on Transsexual Athletes at the 2004
Athens Summer Games, *Body and Society* 12:3 (2006), 75–102.

19 K. Franke, "Gender Verification Tests" in Sport, Feminist Law Professors web
site (September 11, 2009), http://feministlawprofessors.com/?p=12898

20 L. Davis and L. Delano, Fixing the Boundaries of Physical Gender: Side
Effects of Anti-Drug Campaigns in Athletics, *Sociology of Sport Journal* 9:1
(1992), 1–19

21 Ibid.

22 Quoted by Dave Zirin in Women's Gymnastics: The Big Mac of the
Beijing Games, *The Nation* (September 2008), http://www.thenation.com/
signup/18366?destination=blog/womens-gymnastics-big-mac-beijing-games

23 B. Smith, Where Have Our Champion Women Figure Skaters Gone? *Globe
and Mail* (December 6, 1997), D9.

24 Lenskyj, *Olympic Industry Resistance: Challenging Olympic Power and
Propaganda* (Albany, NY: SUNY Press, 2008), 17.

25 A. Jennings, *The New Lords of the Rings* (London: Pocket Books, 1996), 39–40.

26 A. Jennings, Sport, Lies and Stasi-Files – A Golden Opportunity for the
Press, Play the Game web site (June 17, 1997), http://www.playthegame.org/
knowledge-bank/articles/sport-lies-and-stasi-files-a-golden-opportunity-for-
the-press-1040.html

27 IOC factsheet, Women in the Olympic Movement (updated June 2011),
http://www.olympic.org/Documents/Reference_documents_Factsheets/
Women_in_Olympic_Movement.pdf

28 Homosexuals Should "Refrain from Any Sexual Activities" at 2022 World
Cup: FIFA Boss, *Globe and Mail* (December 14, 2010), S5.

29 FIFA Boss Sepp Blatter Sorry for Qatar "Gay" Remarks, BBC Sport web site
(September 17, 2010), http://news.bbc.co.uk/sport2/hi/football/9297497.stm

30 M. Amara and E. Theodoraki, Transnational Network Formation through
Sports Related Regional Development Projects in the Arabian Peninsula,
International Journal of Sport Policy 2:2 (2010), 135–58.

31   See P. Boyle, The Olympics, Security and Urban Governance, in Lenskyj and Wagg, 394–409; Lenskyj, *Inside the Olympic Industry: Power, Politics and Activism* (Albany, NY: SUNY Press, 2000), 108–22.

32   P. Miller, The Nazi Olympics, Berlin, 1936, *Olympika* 5 (1996), 127–40.

33   C. Rutheiser, *Imagineering Atlanta* (New York: Verso, 1996).

34   G. Kinsman and P. Gentile, *Canadian War on Queers* (Vancouver, BC: University of British Columbia Press, 2010), 310.

35   Denis LeBlanc cited in Kinsman and Gentile, 315.

36   Ibid., 310.

37   D. McLeod, Lesbian and Gay Liberation in Canada: A Selected Annotated Bibliography, unpublished draft manuscript (April 25, 2012 version).

38   S. Russell, The Sydney 2000 Olympics and the Game of Political Repression: An Insider's Account, *Canadian Law and Society Journal* 18 (1994), 9–12.

39   G. Cox, M. Darcy, and M Bounds, *The Olympics and Housing* (Sydney: Shelter NSW, 1994).

40   C. Mulling, Dissidents' Perspective of the 1988 Seoul Olympics, in *Toward One World Beyond All Barriers*, Proceedings of Seoul Olympiad Anniversary Conference (Seoul, Korea: Poong Nam Publishing, 1990), 394–407.

41   Jennifer Roemhildt quoted in V. Hayes, Human Trafficking for Sexual Exploitation at World Sporting Events, *Chicago-Kent Law Review* 85:3 (2010), 1106.

42   B. Perrin, *Faster, Higher, Stronger: Preventing Human Trafficking at the 2010 Olympics* (Calgary, AB: The Future Group, 2007), 14.

43   Sex Industry Worker Safety Action Group, *Human Trafficking, Sex Work Safety and the 2010 Games* (Vancouver, June 10, 2009).

44   Hayes, 1139.

45   End Violence Against Women flyer (2012), http://www.endviolenceagainstwomen.org.uk/london-olympics-2012

46   See, for example, M. Young, The IOC Made Me Do It: Women's Ski Jumping, VANOC and the 2010 Olympic Games, *Constitutional Forum* 18:3 (2010), 95–107. This article has 96 footnotes, the majority citing scholarly articles, legal decisions and newspaper coverage of the ski jump trials. For typical coverage in liberal sport feminist media, see A. Murray, Will Women's Ski Jumping Be Included in the 2010 Olympics? *Promotion Plus Network News* 20:1 (2009), 1, 5.

47   A. Travers, Women's Ski Jumping, the 2010 Olympic Games, and the Deafening Silence of Sex Segregation, Whiteness and Wealth, *Journal of Sport and Social Issues* 35:2 (2011), 136.

48   Ibid.

49   Ibid., 137.

50   Ibid., 139.

51   Ibid., 141; see also H. Lenskyj, The Winter Olympics: Geography Is Destiny? in Lenskyj and Wagg, 88–102.

DOI: 10.1057/9781137291158

52   Highway of Tears web site, http://www.highwayoftears.ca/miscnews.htm

53   D. Eby, The Olympics, Housing and Homelessness in Vancouver, Canadian Centre for Policy Alternatives web site (2008), http://www.policyalternatives.ca/publications/commentary/olympics-housing-and-homelessness-vancouver

54   Downtown Eastside Women's Centre web site, http://dewc.ca/about

55   H. Walia quoted in M. Abbs, C. Frampton, and J. Peart (2009), Going for Gold on Stolen Land: A Roundtable on Anti-Olympic Organizing, *Upping the Anti* 9, 152.

56   Murray, 5.

DOI: 10.1057/9781137291158

7
Conclusion

Abstract: *Three main themes – identity construction and the body, symbolic representations and social structures – have shaped my analysis of gender politics and the Olympic industry between 1896 and 2012. A focus on three models of sportive movement – achievement sport, fitness sport and body experience sport – has illustrated the ways in which the Olympic industry privileges certain gendered, classed, raced and sexualized sporting bodies and a limited range of sporting performances. Most Olympic resistance movements have focused on the non-sport impacts on host cities and regions, rather than specific issues of sport and gender. New media offer the possibility of convergence, with activists working together to address social problems exacerbated by the Olympic industry.*

Lenskyj, Helen Jefferson. *Gender Politics and the Olympic Industry*. Basingstoke: Palgrave Macmillan, 2013.
DOI: 10.1057/9781137291158.

Throughout the preceding chapters, I have followed three main themes – identity construction and the body, symbolic representations and social structures – in order to analyse gender politics and the Olympic industry between 1896 and 2012. At the same time, a focus on three models of sportive movement – achievement sport, fitness sport and body experience sport – has illustrated the ways in which the Olympic industry privileges certain gendered, classed, raced and sexualized sporting bodies and a limited range of sporting performances. In doing so, it perpetuates longstanding systems of colonialism and oppression.

Achievement sport, exemplified by the Olympic faster/higher/stronger motto, provides little room for physical activities based on kinaesthetic movement. Thus, the structure of the Olympic sport programme rewards strength and endurance, while marginalizing activities to which smaller, lighter bodies are suited. When male athletes participate in figure skating, a sport that requires strength and endurance as well as graceful and artistic movement, or when female athletes display more muscularity than artistry, their heterosexual identity is likely to be questioned. The Olympic sport programme reflects and entrenches gender boundaries, and the Olympic industry's control over world sport limits the possibilities for men as well as women. Case studies of individual athletes illustrate accommodation or resistance to entrenched gender-related patterns of *being* and *doing*. Some women and men challenged societal norms by performing gender and sport differently, and their individual achievements paved the way for gradually changing representations of the male and female body, both inside and outside sport. At the same time, the female apologetic in women's sport – performances of heterosexual femininity ranging from beauty makeovers to nude poses – undermined the more progressive initiatives, most notably the struggle for sportswomen's recognition solely on the basis of their achievements.

Physical differences based on body type and/or ethnicity result in a wide range of female sporting bodies, including tall, muscular women with impressive successes in achievement sport. Throughout the 20th century, the conservative emphasis on the beauty and grace that female athletes were said to contribute to the Olympic spectacle worked against those women whose bodies did not fit the ideals of hegemonic femininity, as defined in specific historical periods and cultural contexts. If these women were big, strong and Black, they faced additional barriers of racist discrimination and exclusion. The ever-expanding reach of television and the Internet, as well as the print media, brought images of a

DOI: 10.1057/9781137291158

"new woman," the Olympic athlete, to a global audience, but the women who attracted the most positive media attention and gained iconic status had to be "feminine" in appearance and comportment – in other words, conventionally heterosexually attractive. To be labelled "unfeminine" suggested, and continues to suggest, lesbianism, or prompts allegations of steroid use.

Changing the channel: new media

The mainstream media have been largely responsible for creating the official Olympic narratives: celebrating humanity, overcoming adversity, bringing the world together, promoting peace and so on. Since 1984, with the purported financial success of the Los Angeles Games and the competition for media rights holder status, the media's largely uncritical support of all things Olympic has resulted in what Canadian sociologist Varda Burstyn termed "a de facto mainstream media blackout of organized anti-Olympic struggles."[1]

In the 1990s, as new forms of media were developed, activists seized the opportunities offered by the Internet to challenge the Olympic industry propaganda that saturated bid and host cities.[2] Olympic watchdog and anti-Olympic groups around the globe set up web sites and maintained email connections, forming a loose international network and sharing human and material resources. During the Olympics, independent media centres in Sydney and Vancouver were among the many resistance initiatives aimed at circulating the stories behind the official story, with the struggles of Indigenous peoples a key focus. Housing and homelessness problems exacerbated by hosting the Olympics and the threat to basic freedoms of speech and assembly in host cities and countries were universal concerns among all these resistance groups.

As web technologies developed in the past decade to allow user-generated content, citizen journalists were able to send reports, photos and videos directly to web sites. During the 2010 Vancouver Games, for example, the first Olympic social media centre, True North Media House, was established, and served as a prototype for future Games.[3] The threat that this trend posed to Olympic hegemony did not escape attention, and since 2009 the IOC has been intent on harnessing the new media for financial gain, through the monetization of its digital assets.[4] In addition, IOC lawyers have been kept busy tracking down alleged

DOI: 10.1057/9781137291158

copyright infringements of Olympic words and symbols that appear in the alternative media.

By 2012, a wide range of social media initiatives, including Facebook and Twitter, had been developed and used to good effect by anti-globalization, anti-Olympic groups and, since September 2011, Occupy Movements around the world. As British sociologist and activist Jennifer Jones explained in an article titled "Occupying the Olympic Games: Resisting London 2012":

> There is one thing that can't be controlled in terms of the Olympic narrative (and in turn what is archived and remembered) and that is the digital footprint that the Games leave behind...the Occupy London camp may disappear, but its digital trail...will give a more complete story of what has happened...And if such stories can be collected, or at least recognized as important archive resources, there is a greater chance of reclaiming, and therefore occupying the Olympic Games.[5]

Remember gender?

These resistance initiatives have succeeded in raising public awareness of the negative social, economic and environmental impacts of the Olympics, as well as the threats to freedom of speech and freedom of assembly in host countries. Olympic watchdog groups have paid attention to gender issues in relation to housing and homelessness, prostitution and sex trafficking, which are clearly high-priority and ongoing issues in host cities and regions, and the activists' blogs and web sites reflect these concerns. However, gender issues in Olympic *sport* itself tend to be neglected in the new media revolution. There are obviously good reasons for activists to focus on Olympic impacts beyond the actual sporting events that dominate world media every two years, and, without their work, the human tragedies would fade into the background. Yet, with liberal sport feminist groups failing to develop a radical analysis of sport issues, and Olympic watchdog groups focusing on non-sport issues, the bigger topic of gender politics and the Olympic industry is in danger of falling through the cracks.

In April 1999, I attended a meeting of Bondi Olympic Watch, a community group that was opposing the construction of a temporary beach volleyball stadium on the pristine sands of Bondi Beach, in preparation for the Sydney 2000 Olympics. The president of the international

DOI: 10.1057/9781137291158

federation had insisted on this site, primarily to boost the popularity of the sport among international television audiences. The protest focused on the environmental damage and the virtual privatization of a large section of the beach for more than five months. Some attention was paid to the obvious sexploitation of female players, and, as one critic noted, the televised Olympic sport was so popular that it probably could have been held in a parking lot without any impact on viewers.[6] However, Bondi Olympic Watch kept its attention almost exclusively on the social and environmental impacts – that is, the non-sport issues. In a different scenario, one might imagine the environmentalists, community activists and sport feminists working together in a coalition, but WomenSport New South Wales, a liberal sport feminist organization, was an unlikely candidate for an anti-Olympic protest, especially one like this that involved civil disobedience (a sit-in on the beach). The concept of convergence, mentioned earlier in relation to the Vancouver anti-Olympic protests and facilitated by the new social media, has the potential to bring together a wide range of community activists to address social injustice. In an ideal world, these women and men would work together to challenge interlocking systems of oppression that are played out in Olympic sport and perpetuated by the Olympic industry.

For more than 100 years, the Olympic industry has controlled global sport and shaped hegemonic concepts of sporting masculinities and femininities for its own profit- and image-making ends. The potential for exploitation and co-optation of women and disadvantaged minorities is great; the benefits few by comparison. The industry has a long and disturbing history of marginalizing women, Black people and people of colour, athletes from developing countries, working-class people and sexual minorities. Successful alternatives organized by these groups have demonstrated that other ways of doing sport and doing gender are both possible and preferable.

Notes

1   V. Burstyn, Foreword, in H. Lenskyj, *Inside the Olympic Industry: Power, Politics and Activism* (Albany, NY: SUNY Press, 2000), xii.

2   H. Lenskyj, Alternative Media versus the Olympic Industry, in A. Raney and J. Bryant (eds.), *Handbook of Sports and Media* (Mahwah, NJ: Lawrence Erlbaum Associates, 2006), 205–16.

DOI: 10.1057/9781137291158

3   True North Media House web site, http://truenorthmediahouse.com/about/principles/
4   A. Miah and J. Jones, The Olympic Movement's New Media Revolution: Monetization, Open Media and Intellectual Property, in H. Lenskyj and S. Wagg (eds), *Handbook of Olympic Studies* (Basingstoke, UK: Palgrave Macmillan, 2012), 274–88.
5   J. Jones, Occupying the Olympic Games: Resisting London 2012, British Library web site, http://www.bl.uk/sportandsociety/exploresocsci/politics/articles/occupying.pdf
6   Lenskyj, *The Best Olympics Ever? Social Impacts of Sydney 2000* (Albany, NY: SUNY Press, 2002), 186; for a full discussion of these events, see chapter 8 therein.

DOI: 10.1057/9781137291158

Bibliography

Abbs, M., C. Frampton and J. Peart (2009), Going for
   Gold on Stolen Land: A Roundtable on Anti-Olympic
   Organizing, *Upping the Anti* 9, 141–57.

Adams, M. L. (2011) *Artistic Impressions: Figure Skating,
   Masculinity, and the Limits of Sport* (Toronto: University
   of Toronto Press).

Amaechi, D. (2007) *Man in the Middle* (New York: ESPN
   Books).

Amara, M. and E. Theodoraki (2010) Transnational
   Network Formation through Sports Related Regional
   Development Projects in the Arabian Peninsula,
   International Journal of Sport Policy 2:2, 135–58.

Arnold, G. (1998) Synch Different, *Metroactive*. http://
   www.metroactive.com/papers/metro/09.10.98/cover/
   synchroswim-9836.html

Associated Press and Grolier Enterprises (1979) *Pursuit
   of Excellence: The Olympic Story* (Danbury, CT: Grolier
   Enterprises).

Australian Institute of Health and Welfare (2000)
   Australia's Health 2000 (Canberra: AIHW).

Bale, J. (2001) Nyandika Maiyoro and Kipchoge Keino:
   Transgression, Colonial Rhetoric and the Postcolonial
   Athlete, in D. Andrews and S. Jackson (eds), *Sports
   Stars: The Cultural Politics of Sporting Celebrity* (London:
   Routledge), 218–30.

Bandy, S. (2010) Politics of Gender through the
   Olympics, in A. Bairner and G. Molnar (eds),
   The Politics of the Olympics: A Survey (London:
   Routledge), 41–57.

Beijing Olympics Draw Largest Ever Global TV Audience, Neilson Ratings web site (September 5, 2008). http://blog.nielsen.com/nielsenwire/media_entertainment/beijing-olympics-draw-largest-ever-global-tv-audience/

Bell, D. (February 8, 1997) Figure Skating, the Never-Ending Story, *Globe and Mail*, D9.

Blue, A. (1988) *Faster, Higher, Further: Women's Triumphs and Disasters at the Olympics* (London: Virago).

Borish, L. (2009) Charlotte Epstein, *Jewish Women: A Comprehensive Historical Encyclopedia*, Jewish Women's Archive. http://jwa.org/encyclopedia/article/epstein-charlotte

Boyle, P. (2012) The Olympics, Security and Urban Governance, in H. Lenskyj and S. Wagg (eds), *Handbook of Olympic Studies* (Basingstoke, UK: Palgrave Macmillan), 394–409.

Breckenridge, C. (2001) *Spoilsports* (London: Routledge).

Brennan, C. (1997) *Inside Edge* (New York: Knopf Doubleday).

Brohm, J.-M. (1978) *Sport: A Prison of Measured Time*, trans I. Fraser (London: Ink Links).

Buchanan, I. (2000) Asia's First Female Olympian, *Journal of Olympic History* 8:3, 22–3.

Burstyn, V. (2000) Foreword, in H. Lenskyj, *Inside the Olympic Industry: Power, Politics and Activism* (Albany, NY: SUNY Press), i–xiv.

Butler, J. (1990) *Gender Trouble: Feminism and the Subversion of Identity* (New York: Routledge).

Butler, J. (1998) Athletic Genders, *Stanford Humanities Review*, 6:2. http://www.stanford.edu/group/SHR/6-2/html/butler.html

Buzinski, J. and C. Zeigler (2007) *The OutSports Revolution* (New York: Alyson).

CAAWS Presents at the IOC Women and Sport Conference (March 21, 2012), CAAWS web site. http://www.caaws.ca/e/archives/article.cfm?id=4451&search=olympic

Cahn, S. (1994) *Coming on Strong: Gender and Sexuality in Twentieth-Century Women's Sport* (Cambridge, MA: Harvard University Press).

Carlos, J. and D. Zirin (2011) *The John Carlos Story: The Sports Moment That Changed the World* (Chicago, IL: Haymarket Books).

Carpenter, L. and R. Acosta (2005) *Title IX* (Champaign, IL: Human Kinetics).

Carr, S. (2009) Title IX: An Opportunity to Level the Olympic Playing Field, *Seton Hall Journal of Sports and Entertainment Law* 19, 149–80.

DOI: 10.1057/9781137291158

Cashman, R. (2001) Barrackers' Corner: A Rejoinder to a "One-Eyed" Review of *Staging the Olympics*, *Sporting Traditions* 18:1, 127–9.

Caster Semenya, *New York Times* (August 26, 2009). http://topics.nytimes.com/topics/reference/timestopics/people/s/caster_semenya/index.html

Caster Semenya Unveils Glamorous Look, Pink News web site (September 9, 2009). http://www.pinknews.co.uk/2009/09/09/caster-semenya-unveils-glamorous-look-as-she-learns-shell-keep-gold-medal/

Cavanagh, H. S. and H. Sykes (2006) Transsexual Bodies at the Olympics: The International Olympic Committee's Policy on Transsexual Athletes at the 2004 Athens Summer Games, *Body and Society* 12:3, 75–102.

The Chairman of the "Maccabi World Union" Writes to Us (February 1962) *Olympic Review* 77, 45.

Chatziefstathiou, D. (2012) Pierre de Coubertin: Man and Myth, in H. Lenskyj and S. Wagg (eds), *Handbook of Olympic Studies* (Basingstoke, UK: Palgrave Macmillan), 26–40.

Chatziefstathiou, D., I. Henry, E. Theodoraki, and M. Al-Tauqi (2006) Cultural Imperialism and the Diffusion of Olympic Sport in Africa, in N. Crowther, R. Barney, and M. Heine (eds), *Cultural Imperialism in Action: Critiques in the Global Olympic Trust*, Proceedings of the Eighth International Symposium for Olympic Research (London, ON: University of Western Ontario), 278–92.

Chodorow, N. (1989) *Feminism and Psychoanalytic Theory* (New Haven, CT: Yale University Press).

Clark, J. (1994) Realness ... or Sellout? Sanctioned Events in the Gay Games, Joe Clark web site. http://joeclark.org/sanctioning.html

Clay, D., V. Vignoles, and H. Dittmar (2005) Body Image and Self-esteem among Adolescent Girls: Testing the Influence of Sociocultural Factors, *Journal of Research on Adolescence* 15:4, 451–77.

Close, P., D. Askew, and X. Xin (2007) *The Beijing Olympiad* (New York: Routledge).

Coad, D. (2008) *The Metrosexual* (Albany, NY: SUNY Press).

Collier, R. (2011) Genetic Tests for Athletic Ability: Science or Snake Oil? *Canadian Medical Association Journal* 184:1, E43–4.

Colwin, C. (2002) *Breakthrough Swimming* (Champaign, IL: Human Kinetics).

Connell, R. W. (1998) Masculinities and Globalization, *Men and Masculinities* 1:1, 3–23.

DOI: 10.1057/9781137291158

Cosentino, F. and G. Leyshon (1975) *Olympic Gold* (Toronto: Holt, Rinehart and Winston).

Cox, G., M. Darcy, and M. Bounds (1994) *The Olympics and Housing* (Sydney: Shelter NSW).

Crenshaw, K. (1993) Mapping the Margins: Intersectionality, Identity Politics, and Violence against Women of Color, *Stanford Law Review* 43, 1241–99.

Da Costa, N. (January 17, 2004) "I Want Short Shorts": Blatter, *Toronto Star*.

Daddario, G. and B. Wigley (2007) Gender Marking and Racial Stereotyping at the 2004 Athens Games, *Journal of Sports Media* 2:1, 31–51.

Davis, K. (2007) *The Making of Our Bodies Ourselves: How Feminism Travels across Borders* (Durham, NC: Duke University Press).

Davis, L. (1997) *The Swimsuit Issue and Sport* (Albany, NY: SUNY Press).

Davis, L. and L. Delano (1992) Fixing the Boundaries of Physical Gender: Side Effects of Anti-Drug Campaigns in Athletics, *Sociology of Sport Journal* 9:1, 1–19.

De Coubertin, P. (January 1987) "We Want to Go Ever Forward": The Trustees of the Olympic Idea, *Olympic Review*, 46–8. Originally published in *Olympic Review* (July 1908), 108–10.

DeFranz, A. (1993) The Olympic Games: Our Birthright to Sport, in G. Cohen (ed.), *Women in Sport: Issues and Controversies* (Newbury Park, CA: Sage), 185–92.

DePauw, K. (1997) The (In)visibility of Disability: Cultural Contexts and "Sporting Bodies," *Quest* 49, 416–30.

Duncan, M. C. (2006) Gender Warriors in Sport, in A. Raney and J. Bryant (eds), *Handbook of Sports and Media* (Mahwah, NJ: Lawrence Erlbaum Associates), 231–52.

Dyreson, M. (1994) From Civil Rights to Scientific Racism: The Variety of Responses to the Berlin Olympics, the Legend of Jesse Owens and the "Race Question," in R. Barney and K. Meier (eds), *Critical Reflections on Olympic Ideology*, Proceedings of the Second International Symposium for Olympic Research (London, ON: University of Western Ontario), 46–54.

Dyreson, M. (2008) Johnny Weissmuller and the Old Global Capitalism: The Origins of the Federal Blueprint for Selling American Culture to the World, *International Journal of the History of Sport* 25:2, 268–83.

DOI: 10.1057/9781137291158

Eby, D. (2008) The Olympics, Housing and Homelessness in Vancouver, Canadian Centre for Policy Alternatives web site. http://www. policyalternatives.ca/publications/commentary/olympics-housing-and-homelessness-vancouver

Edwards, H. (1973) *Sociology of Sport* (Belmont, CA: Dorsey Press).

Edwards, H. (2000) Crisis of Black Athletes on the Eve of the 21st Century, *Society* 37:3, 9–13.

Eichberg, H. (1998) *Body Cultures* (London: Routledge).

Eichberg, H. (2004) The Global, the Popular and the Inter-popular: Olympic Sport between Market, State and Civil Society, in J. Bale and M. Christensen (eds), *Post Olympism? Questioning Sport in the Twenty-first Century* (London: Berg), 65–80.

Eisen, G. (1979) Olympic Ideology & Jewish Values: Conflict or Accommodation? in R. Barney et al. (eds), *Olympic Perspectives*, Proceedings of the Third International Symposium for Olympic Research (London, ON: University of Western Ontario), 121–6.

Eisen, G. (1998) Jewish History and the Ideology of Modern Sport: Approaches and Interpretations, *Journal of Sport History* 25:3, 482–531.

Espy, R. (1979) *The Politics of the Olympic Games* (Berkeley, CA: University of California Press).

Fanny Blankers-Koen, *Encyclopedia of World Biography* (2004). http://www.encyclopedia.com/topic/Fanny_Blankers-Koen.aspx

Fausto-Sterling, A. (2000) *Sexing the Body* (New York: Basic Books).

Feeney, L. and C. Hickey (dir.) (2006) *Garlic and Watermelons* (Chicago, IL: Pattern Films).

Fellows, M. L. and S. Razack (1998) The Race to Innocence, *Iowa Journal of Race, Gender and Justice* 1:2, 335–52.

Female Beach Volleyball Players Permitted to Wear Less Revealing Uniforms, *The Telegraph* (March 27, 2012). http://www.telegraph. co.uk/sport/olympics/volleyball/9169429/London-2012-Olympics-female-beach-volleyball-players-permitted-to-wear-less-revealing-uniforms.html

FIFA Boss Sepp Blatter Sorry for Qatar "Gay" Remarks, BBC Sport web site (September 17, 2010). http://news.bbc.co.uk/sport2/hi/football/9297497.stm

Fleming, S. and I. McDonald (2001) Racial Science and South Asian and Black Physicality, in B. Carrington (ed.), *Race, Sport and British Society* (London: Routledge), 105–20.

DOI: 10.1057/9781137291158

Franke, K. (September 11, 2009) "Gender Verification Tests" in Sport, Feminist Law Professors web site. http://feministlawprofessors. com/?p=12898

Franklin, U. (1985) Will Women Change Technology or Will Technology Change Women? *CRIAW Papers* (Ottawa: CRIAW).

From Hollywood Gold to Hollywood Glitters (1995) *Olympic Review* 25:2, 50–4.

Galindo, R. with E. Marcus (1997) *Icebreaker* (New York: Pocket Books).

Garber, M. (1995) Victor Petrenko's Mother-in-Law, in C. Baughmann (ed.), *Women on Ice* (New York: Routledge), 93–102.

Gechtman, R. (1999) Socialist Mass Politics through Sport: The Bund's Morgnshtern in Poland, 1926–1939, *Journal of Sport History* 26:2, 346–52.

Giardina, M., J. Metz, and K. Bunds (2012) USA Celebrate Humanity: Cultural Citizenship and the Global Branding of "Multiculturalism," in H. Lenskyj and S. Wagg (eds), *Handbook of Olympic Studies* (Basingstoke, UK: Palgrave Macmillan), 337–57.

Ginnane, M. (dir.) (August 31, 2011) Too Fast to Be a Woman, *The Passionate Eye* (Ottawa: CBC Television).

Giulianotti, R. (2004) Human Rights, Globalization and Sentimental Education: The Case of Sport, *Sport in Society* 7:3, 355–69.

Golden, M. (2012) The Ancient Games and the Modern: Mirror and Mirage, in H. Lenskyj and S. Wagg (eds), *Handbook of Olympic Studies* (Basingstoke, UK: Palgrave Macmillan), 15–25.

Goodhart, P. and C. Chataway (1968) *War without Weapons* (London: Allen).

Gori, G. (2001) "A Glittering Icon of Fascist Femininity": Trebisonda "Ondina" Valla, *International Journal of the History of Sport* 18:1, 173–95.

Griffin, P. (1998) *Strong Women, Deep Closets* (Champaign, IL: Human Kinetics).

Groesz, L., M. Levine, and S. Murnen (2001) The Effect of Experimental Presentation of Thin Media Images on Body Satisfaction: A Meta-analytic Review, *International Journal of Eating Disorders* 31, 1–16.

Guttmann, A. (1992) *The Olympics* (Champaign, IL: University of Illinois Press).

Guttmann, A. (1996) *The Erotic in Sport* (New York: Columbia University Press).

Guttmann, A. (2007) *Sports: The First Five Millennia* (Amherst, MA: University of Massachusetts Press).

DOI: 10.1057/9781137291158

Hall, M. A. (2002) *The Girl and the Game* (Toronto: University of Toronto Press).

Hall Collins, P. (1990) *Black Feminist Thought* (New York: Routledge).

Hattenstone, S. (May 4, 2012) Town of Champions, *Guardian Weekly*, 25–7.

Hayes, V. (2010) Human Trafficking for Sexual Exploitation at World Sporting Events, *Chicago-Kent Law Review* 85:3, 1105–46.

Hill, G. (2003) They Love Everything about Indigenous Peoples, Except the People, Vancouver Media Co-op web site (posted October 27, 2009). http://vancouver.mediacoop.ca/audio/2003

Hoberman, J. (1997) *Darwin's Athletes* (New York: Houghton Mifflin).

Homosexuals Should "Refrain from Any Sexual Activities" at 2022 World Cup: FIFA Boss (December 14, 2010), *Globe and Mail*, S5.

Hong, F. (2004) Innocence Lost: Child Athletes in China, *Sport in Society* 7.3, 338–54.

Hoose, P. (1989) *Necessities: Racial Barriers in American Sports* (New York: Random House).

Hughson, S. (1998) The Bodysuit: Empowering or Objectifying Australia's Elite Women Athletes? unpublished paper (Canberra: Psychology Department, Australian Institute of Sport).

Human Rights Watch (2012), "Steps of the Devil": Denial of Women and Girls' Right to Sport in Saudi Arabia. http://www.hrw.org/sites/default/files/reports/saudi0212webwcover.pdf

Huntsman, L. (2001) *Sand in Our Souls* (Melbourne: Melbourne University Press).

Independent Sport Panel (2009) *The Future of Sport in Australia* (Canberra: Commonwealth of Australia).

James, R. (2011) Genitals to Genes: The History and Biology of Gender Verification in the Olympics, *Canadian Bulletin of Medical History* 28:2 339–65.

James, S. (February 19, 2010) Brother-Sister Skating Pairs, Too Close for Comfort, ABC News web site. http://abcnews.go.com/Health/Olympics/olympic-brother-sister-skating-pairs-close-vancouver-ice/story?id=9887494

Jennings, A. (1996) *The New Lords of the Rings* (London: Pocket Books).

Jennings, A. (June 17, 1997) Sport, Lies and Stasi-Files – A Golden Opportunity for the Press, Play the Game web site. http://www.playthegame.org/knowledge-bank/articles/sport-lies-and-stasi-files-a-golden-opportunity-for-the-press-1040.html

DOI: 10.1057/9781137291158

Jennings, A. (July 17, 2000) Silver Tongues and Olympic Gold, *Sydney Morning Herald*.

Johnson, D. and A. Ali (2004) A Tale of Two Seasons, *Social Science Quarterly* 85:4, 974–93.

Johnson, L. (2004) Women Writing on Physical Culture in Pre-Civil War Catalonia, working paper (Berkeley, CA: Institute of European Studies, University of California, Berkeley). http://escholarship.org/uc/item/0bc654jh

Jones, J. (2012) Occupying the Olympic Games: Resisting London 2012, British Library web site. http://www.bl.uk/sportandsociety/exploresocsci/politics/articles/occupying.pdf

Jutel, A. (2003) "Thou Dost Run As in Flotation": Femininity, Reassurance and the Emergence of the Women's Marathon, *International Journal of the History of Sport* 20:3, 17–36.

Kaufman, K. (February 22, 2002) So They're All Gay, Right? Salon.com web site. http://www.salon.com/2002/02/22/galindo/

Kidd, B. (1984) The Myth of the Ancient Games, in A. Tomlinson and G. Whannel (eds), *Five Ring Circus: Money, Power and Politics at the Olympic Games* (London: Pluto), 71–83.

Kinsman, G. and P. Gentile (2010) *Canadian War on Queers* (Vancouver, BC: University of British Columbia Press).

Kjeldsen, E. (1984) Integration of Minorities into Olympic Sport in Canada and the USA, *Journal of Sport and Social Issues* 8:2, 30–44.

Kling, K., J. Hyde, C. Showers, and B. Buswell (1999) Gender Differences in Self-esteem: A Meta-analysis, *Psychological Bulletin* 125:4, 470–500.

Lackey, D. (1990) Sexual Harassment in Sports, *Physical Educator* 47:2, 22–6.

Lafrance, M. (1999) What's the Problem? *Canadian Issues* 1:1, 20–2.

Large, D. (2012) The Nazi Olympics: Berlin 1936, in H. Lenskyj and S. Wagg (eds), *Handbook of Olympic Studies* (Basingstoke, UK: Palgrave Macmillan), 60–71.

Larmer, B. (2005) *Operation Yao Ming* (New York: Gotham Books).

Leigh, M. and T. Bonin (1977) The Pioneering Role of Madame Alice Milliat and the FSFI, *Journal of Sport History* 4:1, 72–83.

Lekarska, N. (1973) *Essays and Studies on Olympic Problems* (Sofia: Medicina and Fitzcultura).

Lenskyj, H. (1983) "We Want to Play, We'll Play": Women and Sport in the Twenties and Thirties. *Canadian Women's Studies* 4:3, 15–18.

DOI: 10.1057/9781137291158

Lenskyj, H. (1986) *Out of Bounds: Women, Sport and Sexuality* (Toronto: Women's Press).

Lenskyj, H. (2002) *The Best Olympics Ever? Social Impacts of Sydney 2000* (Albany, NY: SUNY Press).

Lenskyj, H. (2003) *Out on the Field: Gender, Sport and Sexualities* (Toronto: Women's Press).

Lenskyj, H. (2006) Alternative Media versus the Olympic Industry, in A. Raney and J. Bryant (eds), *Handbook of Sports and Media* (Mahwah, NJ: Lawrence Erlbaum Associates), 205–16.

Lenskyj, H. (2006) I Am My Body: Challenge and Change in Girls' Physical and Health Education, in D. Gustafson and L. Goodyear (eds), *Women, Health and Education* (St Johns, NL: Memorial University), 68–73.

Lenskyj, H. (2008) *Olympic Industry Resistance: Challenging Olympic Power and Propaganda* (Albany, NY: SUNY Press).

Lenskyj, H. (2010) Olympic Power, Olympic Politics: Behind the Scenes, in A. Bairner and G. Molnar (eds), *The Politics of the Olympics* (London: Routledge), 15–26.

Lenskyj, H. (2012) The Winter Olympics: Geography Is Destiny? in H. Lenskyj and S. Wagg (eds), *Handbook of Olympic Studies* (Basingstoke, UK: Palgrave Macmillan), 88–102.

Lenskyj, H. and S. Wagg (eds) (2012) *Handbook of Olympic Studies* (Basingstoke, UK: Palgrave Macmillan).

Levy, J., D. Rosenburg, and D. Hyman (1999) Fanny "Bobbie" Rosenfeld: Canada's Woman Athlete of the Half Century, *Journal of Sport History* 26:2, 392–6.

Llewellyn, M. (2011) The Curse of the Shamateur, *International Journal of the History of Sport* 28:5, 796–816.

Lopiano, D. (1984) A Political Analysis of the Possibility of Impact Alternatives for the Accomplishment of Feminist Objectives within American Intercollegiate Sport, *Arena Review* 8:2, 49–61.

Lorde, A. (1984) The Master's Tools Will Never Dismantle the Master's House, in *Sister Outsider* (Santa Cruz, CA: Crossing Press), 110–13.

Louis-Jacques, T. (February 14, 2012) Black History Month: Louise Stokes, Malden Patch web site. http://malden.patch.com/articles/black-history-month-louise-stokes-fraser

Lowery, S., S. Robinson, C. Kurplus, E. Blanks, S. Sollenerger, M. Nicpon, and L. Huser (2005) Body Image, Self-esteem, and Health-

DOI: 10.1057/9781137291158

Related Behaviors among Male and Female First Year College Students, *Journal of College Student Development* 46:6, 612–23.

Loxley, J. (2007) *Performativity* (London: Routledge).

Lunt, D. and M. Dyreson, (2012) The 1904 Olympic Games: Triumph or Nadir? in H. Lenskyj and S. Wagg (eds), *Handbook of Olympic Studies* (Basingstoke, UK: Palgrave Macmillan), 43–59.

The Maccabiah Games, International Jewish Sports Hall of Fame web site. http://www.jewishsports.net/the_maccabiah_games.htm

Macfarlane, B. (October 2009) Greatest Female Hockey Player of the 1920s, It Happened in Hockey web site. http://www.ithappenedinhockey.com/2009/10/greatest-female-hockey-player-of-the-1920s/

Maguire, J., S. Barnard, K. Butler, and P. Golding (2008) Olympic Legacies in the IOC's "Celebrate Humanity" Campaign: Ancient or Modern? *International Journal of the History of Sport* 25:14, 2041–59.

Mandell, R. (1971) *The Nazi Olympics* (Chicago, IL: University of Illinois Press).

Mangan, J. and R. Park (eds) (1987) *From Fair Sex to Feminism* (London: Cass).

McDonald, M. (2006) Beyond the Pale: The Whiteness of Sport Studies and Queer Scholarship, in J. Hargreaves (ed.), *Sport, Sexualities and Queer Theory* (London: Routledge), 33–45.

McGreal, C. (February 21, 2002) Coming Home, *The Guardian*. http://www.guardian.co.uk/education/2002/feb/21/internationaleducationnews.highereducation

McLeod, D. (April 25, 2012) Lesbian and Gay Liberation in Canada: A Selected Annotated Bibliography, unpublished draft manuscript.

Meacham, S. (October 18, 2003) Too Close for Comfort, *Sydney Morning Herald*, 36.

Melloy, K. (July 30, 2008) No Olympic Glory for Male Synchronized Swimmers, *Edge Boston*. http://www.edgeboston.com/index.php?ch=news&sc=glbt&sc2=news&sc3=&id=78177

Merck, M. (March/April 2010) The Question of Caster Semenya, *Radical Philosophy* 180, 2–7.

Miah, A. and J. Jones (2012) The Olympic Movement's New Media Revolution: Monetization, Open Media and Intellectual Property, in H. Lenskyj and S. Wagg (eds), *Handbook of Olympic Studies* (Basingstoke, UK: Palgrave Macmillan), 274–88.

Miller, P. (1996) The Nazi Olympics, Berlin, 1936, *Olympika* 5, 127–40.

DOI: 10.1057/9781137291158

Miller, T. (1998) Commodifying the Male Body, Problematizing "Hegemonic Masculinity"? *Journal of Sport and Social Issues* 22:4, 431–47.

Miller, T. (2001) *SportSex* (Philadelphia, PA: Temple University Press).

Miller, T., G. Lawrence, J. McKay, and D. Rowe (2001) *Globalization and Sport: Playing the World* (London: Sage).

Miragaya, A. and L. DaCosta (n.d.) Olympic Entrepreneurs – Alice Milliat: The 1st Woman Olympic Entrepreneur, Autonomous University of Barcelona Center for Olympic Studies web site. http://olympicstudies.uab.es/brasil/pdf/8.pdf

Morrow, D. (2002) Olympic Masculinity, in K. Wamsley et al. (eds), *The Global Nexus Engaged*, Proceedings of the Sixth International Symposium for Olympic Research (London, ON: University of Western Ontario), 123–34.

Mulling, C. (1990) Dissidents' Perspective of the 1988 Seoul Olympics, in *Toward One World Beyond All Barriers*, Proceedings of Seoul Olympiad Anniversary Conference (Seoul, Korea: Poong Nam Publishing), 294–407.

Murray, A. (2009) Will Women's Ski Jumping Be Included in the 2010 Olympics? *Promotion Plus Network News* 20:1, 1, 5.

Narvaez, A. (1978) The Fiftieth Anniversary of Women's Participation in Olympic Athletics, *Olympic Review* 134, 701.

National Geographic (2000) *Swimsuits: A Hundred Years of Pictures* (Washington DC: National Geographic Society).

NBC Apologizes for Mitcham Gay Snub, OutSports.com web site (September 27, 2008). http://outsports.com/olympics2008/2008/08/27/nbc-apologizes-for-mitcham-gay-snub/

NBC Defends Not Saying Mitcham Is Gay, OutSports.com web site (September 25, 2008). http://outsports.com/olympics2008/2008/08/25/nbc-defends-not-saying-mitcham-is-gay/

Nendel, J. (2004) New Hawaiian Monarchy: The Media Representations of Duke Kahanamoku, 1911–1912, *Journal of Sport History* 31:1, 32–52.

O'Bonsawin, C. (2004) An Indian Atmosphere, in K. Wamsley et al. (eds), *Cultural Relations Old and New: The Transitory Olympic Ethos*, Proceedings of the Seventh International Symposium for Olympic Research (London, ON: University of Western Ontario), 105–11.

O'Bonsawin, C. (2006) The Conundrum of Ilanaaq: First Nations Representation and the 2010 Vancouver Winter Olympics, in N.

DOI: 10.1057/9781137291158

Crowther, R. Barney, and M. Heine (eds), *Cultural Imperialism in Action: Critiques in the Global Olympic Trust* (London, ON: University of Western Ontario), 387–94.

Olympic Boxing Authority to Discuss Women Wearing Skirts, *TSN* (November 4, 2011). http://www.tsn.ca/story/?id=379674

OutSports.com discussion board (February 11, 13, 2010). http://www.outsports.com/forums/index.php?showtopic=41887

Paradis, L. (2010) Manly Displays: Exhibitions and the Revival of the Olympic Games, *The International Journal of the History of Sport* 27:16–18, 2710–30.

Paraschak, V. (1988) Review of H. Lenskyj, *Out of Bounds, Sport History Review* 19:1, 85–8.

Participation of Women in the Olympic Games, *Official Bulletin of the International Olympic Committee* 28, May 1935.

Perrin, B. (2007) *Faster, Higher, Stronger: Preventing Human Trafficking at the 2010 Olympics* (Calgary, AB: The Future Group).

Pfister, G. and T. Niewerth (1999) Gymnastics and Sport in Germany, *Journal of Sport History* 26:2, 287–325.

Picard, A. (February 15, 1994) Skating with an Olympic-Sized Dream, *Globe and Mail*, A7.

Pound, R. (2006) *Inside Dope* (Mississauga, ON: Wiley).

Pronger, B. (1990) *The Arena of Masculinity: Sports, Homosexuality, and the Meaning of Sex* (New York: St Martin's Press).

Pronger, B. (2002) *Body Fascism* (Toronto: University of Toronto Press).

Raszeja, V. (1992) *A Decent and Proper Exertion: The Rise of Women's Competitive Swimming in Sydney to 1912* (Australian Society for Sports History, Faculty of Arts and Social Sciences, University of Western Sydney).

Rawi, M. (December 22, 2011) Sporting Calendar Girls! Team GB Model for Charity Shoot Ahead of 2012 Olympics, *Daily Mail*. http://www.dailymail.co.uk/femail/article-2076668/London-2012-Olympics-Girls-team-GB-model-lingerie-charity-calendar.html

Reischer, E. and K. Koo (2004) The Body Beautiful: Symbolism and Agency in the Social World, *Annual Review of Anthropology* 33, 297–317.

Riordan, J. (1984) The Workers' Olympics, in A. Tomlinson and G. Whannel (eds), *Five Ring Circus: Money, Power and Politics at the Olympic Games* (London: Pluto), 98–112.

DOI: 10.1057/9781137291158

Rivenburgh, N. (2002) The Olympic Games: Twenty-First Century Challenges As a Global Media Event, *Culture, Sport, Society* 5:3, 31–50.

Rogers, T. (February 15, 2010) Can Figure Skating Go Butch? Salon.com web site. http://www.salon.com/2010/02/15/elvis_stojko_interview/

Role on TV "Tarzan" Makes Rafer Johnson a Bad Guy, *Baltimore Afro-American* (July 19, 1966). http://news.google.com/newspapers?ni d=2205&dat=19660719&id=K8IlAAAAIBAJ&sjid=HPUFAAAAIBAJ &pg=988,3439270

Rounds, K. (May/June 1994) Ice: Reflections on a Sport Out of Whack, *Ms.*, 26–33.

Rowe, D. and G. Lawrence (1986) Nationalism and the Olympics, in D. Rowe and G. Lawrence (eds), *Power Play* (Sydney: Iremonger), 196–203.

Russell, S. (1994) The Sydney 2000 Olympics and the Game of Political Repression: An Insider's Account, *Canadian Law and Society Journal* 18, 9–12.

Rutheiser, C. (1996) *Imagineering Atlanta* (New York: Verso).

Ryan, J. (1995) *Little Girls in Pretty Boxes: The Making and Breaking of Elite Gymnasts and Figure Skaters* (New York: Doubleday).

Saghir, M. and E. Robbins (1973) *Male and Female Homosexuality* (Baltimore, MD: Williams & Wilkins).

Saleem, R. (2010) The Olympic Meddle: The International Olympic Committee's Intrusion of Athletes' Privacy through the Discriminatory Practice of Gender Verification Testing, *John Marshall Journal of Computer and Information Law* 28, 49. http://www.jcil.org/journal/articles/537.html

Sands, R. (2002) *Sport Ethnography* (Champaign, IL: Human Kinetics).

Schantz, O. and K. Gilbert (2012) The Paralympic Movement: Empowerment or Disempowerment for People with Disabilities? in H. Lenskyj and S. Wagg (eds), *Handbook of Olympic Studies* (Basingstoke, UK: Palgrave Macmillan), 358–80.

Schultz, J. (2012) Disciplining Sex: "Gender Verification" Policies and Women's Sport, in H. Lenskyj and S. Wagg (eds), *Handbook of Olympic Studies* (Basingstoke, UK: Palgrave Macmillan), 443–60.

Schweinbenz, A. and A. Cronk (2010) Femininity Control at the Olympic Games, *Third Space* 9:2. http://www.thirdspace.ca/journal/article/view/schweinbenzcronk

DOI: 10.1057/9781137291158

Scott, Rose (1847–1925), *Australian Dictionary of Biography* (n.d.). http://adb.anu.edu.au/biography/scott-rose-8370

Scott, S. (2010) How to Look Good (Nearly) Naked: Regulation of the Swimmer's Body, *Body & Society* 16:2, 143–68.

Sex Industry Worker Safety Action Group (June 10, 2009) *Human Trafficking, Sex Work Safety and the 2010 Games* (Vancouver: SIWSAG).

Shaw, C. (2008) *Five Ring Circus* (Vancouver: New Society).

Sheppard, J. (May 18, 2012) Gove Decries Public Schoolboy Dominance, *Guardian Weekly*, 16.

Smith, B. (December 6, 1997) Where Have Our Champion Women Figure Skaters Gone? *Globe and Mail*, D9.

Smith, D. (2009) Caster Semenya Row: "Who Are White People to Question the Makeup of an African Girl? It Is Racism," *The Observer*. http://www.guardian.co.uk/sport/2009/aug/23/caster-semenya-athletics-gender

Steinem, G. (July 1994) The Strongest Woman in the World, *New Woman*, 69–73.

Stell, M. (1992) *Half the Race: A History of Australian Women in Sport* (North Ryde, NSW: HarperCollins).

Stowers, D. and M. Durm (1996) Does Self-concept Depend on Body Image? A Gender Analysis, *Psychological Reports* 78:2, 643–6.

Suchet, A., D. Jorand, and J. Tuppen (2010) History and Geography of a Forgotten Olympic Project: The Spring Games, *Sport in History* 30:4, 570–87.

Swimming's Touchy Issue, *Sydney Morning Herald* (September 20, 2003).

Swimwear Historical Timeline (n.d.), GlamourSurf web site. http://www.glamoursurf.com/swimwear_timeline.html

Sykes, H. (2006) Transsexual and Transgender Policies in Sport, *Women in Sport and Physical Activity Journal* 15:1, 3–12.

Tatz, C. (1987) *Aborigines in Sport*, Australian Society for Sport History No. 3 (Adelaide: Flinders University).

Teetzel, S. (2006). Equality, Equity, and Inclusion: Issues in Women and Transgendered Athletes' Participation at the Olympics, in N. Crowther, M. Heine, and R. K. Barney (eds), *Cultural Imperialism in Action: Critiques in the Global Olympic Trust*, Proceedings of the Eighth International Symposium for Olympic Research (London, ON: University of Western Ontario), 331–8.

DOI: 10.1057/9781137291158

Terret, T. (2010) From Alice Milliat to Marie-Therese Eyquem: Revisiting Women's Sport in France (1920s–1960s), *International Journal of the History of Sport* 27:7, 1154–72.

Theberge, N. (2000) *Higher Goals* (Albany, NY: SUNY Press).

Tiggemann, M. (2005) Body Dissatisfaction and Adolescent Self-esteem: Prospective Findings, *Body Image* 2, 129–35.

Traikos, M. (March 12, 2012) NHL Misses the Point on Concussions, *National Post*. http://sports.nationalpost.com/2012/03/12/michael-traikos-nhl-gms-just-fine-with-status-quo-on-concussions/

Trangbaek, E. (October 1996) Danish Women Gymnasts: An Olympic Success Story, *Olympic Perspectives*, 237–44.

Travers, A. (2011) Women's Ski Jumping, the 2010 Olympic Games, and the Deafening Silence of Sex Segregation, Whiteness and Wealth, *Journal of Sport and Social Issues* 35:2, 126–45.

Tucker, R. and J. Dugas (August 12, 2008) What Price for an Olympic Gold? The Science of Sport web site. http://www.sportsscientists.com/2008/08/beijing-olympic-medal-price.html

TV Crew Upsets Gay Rights Group, *Toronto Star* (February 21, 2010).

Van Natta Jr, D. (2011) Babe Didrikson Zaharias's Legacy Fades, *New York Times*. http://www.nytimes.com/2011/06/26/sports/golf/babe-didrikson-zahariass-legacy-fades.html?pagewanted=all

Volkwein, K. (1992) Sport and Ethics in Unified Germany – A Critical Analysis, in R. Barney and K. Meier (eds), Proceedings of the First International Symposium for Olympic Research (London ON: University of Western Ontario), 55–66.

Wagg, S. (2012) Tilting at Windmills? Olympic Politics and the Spectre of Amateurism, in H. Lenskyj and S. Wagg (eds), *Handbook of Olympic Studies* (Basingstoke, UK: Palgrave Macmillan), 321–37.

Wallechinsky, D. (1984) *Complete Book of the Olympics* (Harmondsworth, UK: Penguin).

Wamsley, K. and G. Schultz (2000) Rogues and Bedfellows: The IOC and the Incorporation of the FSFI, in K. Wamsley et al. (eds), *Bridging Three Centuries*, Proceedings of the Fifth International Symposium for Olympic Research (London ON: University of Western Ontario), 113–18.

Warner, M. (1991) Fear of a Queer Planet, *Social Text* 29, 3–17.

Warren, P. (2006) *The Lavender Locker Room* (Beverly Hills, CA: Wildcat Press).

DOI: 10.1057/9781137291158

Wiggins, D. (1989) "Great Speed but Little Stamina": The Historical Debate over Black Athletic Superiority, *Journal of Sport History* 16:2, 158–85.

Winker G. and N. Degele (2011) Intersectionality As Multi-Level Analysis: Dealing with Social Inequality, *European Journal of Women's Studies* 18:1, 51–66.

World Champ Semenya's Gender Mystery Solved, *The Age* (September 11, 2009). http://www.theage.com.au/world/world-champ-semenyas-gender-mystery-solved-20090911-fjjq.html

Yallop, R. (October 23, 2003) Intimacy and betrayal, *The Australian*.

Young, I. (1980) Throwing Like a Girl: A Phenomenology of Feminine Body Comportment, Motility and Spatiality, *Human Studies* 3, 137–56.

Young, M. (2010) The IOC Made Me Do It: Women's Ski Jumping, VANOC and the 2010 Olympic Games, *Constitutional Forum* 18:3, 95–107.

Zervas, C. (2012) Anti-Olympic Campaigns, in H. Lenskyj and S. Wagg (eds), *Handbook of Olympic Studies* (Basingstoke, UK: Palgrave Macmillan), 533–48.

Ziemer, T. (September 1, 2008) Out of Sync: Male Synchro Swimmer Banned from Olympics, ABC News web site. http://www.tracyziemer.com/ABC-NEWS-out-of-sync.htm

Zirin, D. (September 2008) Women's Gymnastics: The Big Mac of the Beijing Games, *The Nation*. http://www.thenation.com/signup/18366?destination=blog/womens-gymnastics-big-mac-beijing-games

DOI: 10.1057/9781137291158

Index

Aboriginal peoples, Australia, 21, 22, 44, 53, 59, 60–1, 65, 133

abuse, 29, 44, 60, 65, 91, 112, 118, 123

academics, researchers, 4, 17–19, 31, 32, 34, 44, 122, 123

achievement model, 22, 25, 65

activists, activism, 3, 46, 61, 91, 97, 119–26, 133, 134, 135

adolescence, 17, 29, 63, 76, 91, 93, 97

advocates, advocacy, 3, 18, 29, 45, 69, 122–3, 126

aerobics, 21, 54

Africa, African, 21, 60

African Americans, 8, 23, 30, 31–3, 59, 71, 77–9, 95

African Games, 21, 54

aggression, 25, 65, 93, 115

Amaechi, John, 104

amateurism, 21, 23, 59, 71

"Amazon," 64, 110

American Athletic Union, 67, 69, 124

American Olympic Committee (AOC), 57, 66, 78

Amsterdam 1928 Summer Olympic Games, 69, 70, 73, 76, 77, 99, 113

Ancient Olympic Games, 23, 61, 62

Anthropology Days, 60

anti-Olympic and Olympic watchdog organizations, 3, 53, 133–5

Antwerp 1920 Summer Olympic Games, 67

archery, 64, 70

artistry, 28, 99, 117, 132

Athens 2004 Summer Olympic Games, 61, 92, 96, 114, 122

Atlanta 1996 Summer Olympic Games, 46, 93, 120

Australia, Australians, 3, 4, 13, 16, 21, 22, 28, 29, 31, 33, 43, 47, 53, 59, 60, 61, 64–7, 68, 69, 73, 74, 78, 88–9, 92, 93, 95, 97, 101, 111, 113, 121

Barcelona 1992 Summer Olympic Games, 57, 121

baseball, 59, 71, 104

basketball, 31, 46, 47, 70, 71, 80, 104

beach volleyball, 46–7, 48, 134

"beauty and grace," 62, 63, 73, 80, 90, 104, 132

beauty makeovers, 72, 74

Beijing 2008 Summer Olympic Games, 15, 34, 67, 97, 116

Berlin 1936 Summer Olympic Games, 22, 32, 57, 60, 67, 71, 74, 76, 77, 119

biology, biological, 12, 14, 25, 112
Blatter, Sepp, 47, 118
body experience model, 7, 8, 21, 22, 25, 26, 65, 132
body image, 7, 16–18
body type, 20, 90, 115, 132
bodybuilding, 16, 43
bodysuits, 47, 89
bourgeois sport/values, 20, 55, 58
boycotts, 53, 57, 78
Boyle, Raelene, 73, 111
boys, 12, 16, 17, 24, 25, 26, 59, 91, 94, 97, 101, 103, 104
breasts, 18, 63, 109, 115, 116
bribery, corruption, 3, 22, 53, 117
Brohm, Jean-Marie, 20, 22
brothels, 122, 123
Brundage, Avery, 57, 59, 78
Butler, Judith, 7, 14–16, 113

Canada, Canadian, 2, 3, 5, 21, 22, 25, 28, 31, 33, 40, 41, 42, 45, 48, 53, 54, 60, 61, 69, 70, 71, 72, 73, 88, 92, 93, 97, 101, 102, 103, 110, 117, 120, 121, 123, 124, 125, 126, 133
Canadian Association for the Advancement of Women and Sport and Physical Activity (CAAWS), 31, 41, 45
capitalism, 20, 26, 27, 28, 55
Carlos, John, 78–9
children, 9, 24, 29, 31, 33, 55, 59, 60, 63, 66, 74, 79, 91, 94, 96, 97, 99, 101, 103, 119, 122, 126
China, Chinese, 31, 67, 91, 94, 96, 97, 116
Chodorow, Nancy, 7, 12, 14
choreographers, 99, 100, 101, 102
chromosomes, 26, 111, 113
civil rights, 53, 80, 95
classism, 19, 40, 99, 125
closing ceremony, 61, 62
coaches, coaching, 13, 24, 29, 32, 41, 42, 59, 65, 67, 71, 79, 91–9, 101, 102, 111, 116

colonization, colonialism, 21, 32, 33, 42, 43, 60, 88, 132
Comaneci, Nadia, 116
commodification, 21, 26, 45
conservative politics, 47, 48, 62, 66, 90, 114, 132
cultural studies, 2, 3, 4, 7, 12
cycling, 23, 57

dance, 21, 24, 25, 54, 60, 61, 100
de Coubertin, Pierre, 20, 23, 62, 64, 68
decolonization, 21, 53
democracy, 22, 53, 77, 97, 124
democratization of sport, 8, 53, 55, 58–61
developing countries, 8, 42, 135
Didrikson, Mildred, 71–4
disability, 6, 18, 53
discrimination, oppression, 3, 9, 12, 18, 19, 42–5, 57, 59, 61, 71, 109, 113, 114, 118, 126, 132, 135
diving, 71, 93, 97
doctors, 15, 32, 94, 111, 112
dress, 24, 46, 47, 48, 64, 65, 72, 89, 90, 104
drug testing, 94, 112
Dryden, Nikki, 4, 41, 90, 91, 92, 93, 104

Eastern Europe, Eastern European, 91, 116, 122
economic issues, 32, 45, 75, 94, 100, 134
education, 4, 28, 34, 61, 126
Edwards, Harry, 32, 33, 78–80
"effeminate" male athletes, 26, 98, 101, 102
Eichberg, Henning, 7, 19–21, 22, 24, 26, 34
England, English, 5, 20, 24, 68, 88, 89, 95, 99, 104, 113, 120
environmental issues, 3, 134, 135
Epstein, Charlotte, 67
equal Olympic opportunity, 7, 18, 41, 43, 126
equality, 12, 40, 42, 43, 124
ethics, 31, 33, 56, 91, 117

DOI: 10.1057/9781137291141

ethnic minorities, 6, 7, 42, 54, 59, 61, 67, 94, 117
ethnicity, 2, 3, 5, 18, 19, 22, 23, 32, 34, 40, 64, 80, 126, 132
eugenics, 31–2
Europe, 24, 53, 55, 56, 57, 69, 88, 96, 99, 113
European gymnastics, 21, 54
exclusion, 8, 9, 19, 59, 61, 62, 70, 71, 79, 80, 104, 124, 132
experts, 5, 15, 26, 31, 62, 109, 113, 114
exploitation, 9, 19, 28, 29, 46, 48, 65, 109, 126, 135

fair play, 34, 55, 62
fascism, 53, 57, 76, 77
Fédération Internationale de Natation Association (FINA), 89, 94, 96
Fédération Sportive Féminine Internationale (FSFI), 67–9
female apologetic, 13, 96, 132
feminine, femininities, 12–17, 22, 25–8, 46, 49, 57, 58, 63, 71–5, 76, 79, 90, 99, 102, 104, 109, 115, 132, 135
feminist, feminism, 2, 3, 5, 9, 12, 14, 18, 19, 27, 29, 40–5, 47, 57, 58, 65, 66, 79, 91, 109, 114, 123–6, 134, 135
fencing, 23, 64, 65, 80
festivals, 6, 25, 105
field hockey, 46, 47
FIFA (Fédération Internationale de Football Association), 47, 118, 122
figure skating, 5, 8, 13, 24, 26, 64, 70, 81, 88, 96, 99–104, 117, 132
Finland, Finnish, 31, 75, 90, 117
fitness, 7, 8, 21, 22, 25, 27, 54, 62, 65, 132
folk games/traditions, 21, 54
France, French, 15, 20, 67, 68, 69, 120
Fraser, Dawn, 13, 75
freedom of assembly, 21, 134
freedom of speech, 21, 134
Freeman, Cathy, 22

Galindo, Rudy, 101–2
Gay Games, 8, 9, 30, 54, 88, 96, 98, 100, 103, 105, 114

gay men, 6, 7, 18, 25, 29, 30, 53, 101, 102, 103, 118–21
"gay stigma," 96, 97, 103
gender binaries, 9, 12, 26, 48, 104, 114, 115
gender parity, 40, 43, 117
gender testing, 9, 16, 26, 41, 109, 111–14
genetics, 26, 31, 55, 112, 113, 114
geography, 80, 100, 119
Germany, German, 31, 55, 57, 76, 91, 94, 98, 112, 119, 122
girls, 9, 16, 17, 25, 27, 40, 46, 48, 62, 63, 72, 90, 91, 94, 96, 109, 116, 117
globalization, 2, 32, 53, 134
golf, 70, 71, 72, 80, 99
Great Britain, British, 24, 27, 28, 31, 47, 62, 63, 67, 68, 69, 88, 96, 99, 104, 110, 123, 124, 134
Greece, Greek, 28, 62, 63, 122
Guttmann, Allen, 5, 28, 29, 58, 59, 77, 90
gymnastics, 20, 23, 24, 46, 62, 63, 64, 70, 91, 93, 116, 117

hairstyles, women's, 16, 46, 72, 73, 90, 95, 98, 104, 109, 112, 115
health issues, 15, 21, 26, 28, 44, 69, 94, 110, 113, 114, 115
hegemonic femininity, 15, 17, 18, 46, 58, 62, 64, 98, 105, 109, 132
hegemonic masculinity, 13, 15, 22, 25, 26, 135
Henie, Sonja, 29, 76, 99
heteronormativity, 2, 8, 13, 15, 19, 74, 98, 100, 104
heterosexual attractiveness, 13, 17, 45, 76, 133
high jump, 68, 73, 90, 112
high-performance sport/athletes, 3, 4, 41, 44, 55, 79, 90, 92, 94, 97, 101, 112
Hispanic, 48, 99, 102
Hitler, Adolf, 57, 71, 112
HIV/AIDS, 101, 102
Hollywood films, 28, 59, 76, 77, 80, 99

DOI: 10.1057/9781137291141

homeless people, homelessness, 9, 109, 119–21, 125–6
homophobia, "gay stigma," 9, 26, 30, 31, 40, 45, 72, 74, 96, 97, 99–104, 110
hormones, hormone therapy, 113–15
human rights, 3, 4, 41, 48, 67, 78, 121, 123, 125

ice hockey, 25, 46, 101, 103, 104
identity construction, 7, 8, 12, 19, 34, 58, 88, 132
image, 13, 15, 17, 22, 46, 62, 63, 69, 72, 77, 96, 98, 99, 101, 104, 119, 120, 135
immigrants, 72, 73, 99, 126
Indigenous peoples/Native peoples, 5, 6, 7, 8, 18, 21, 42, 48, 53, 54, 59, 60–1, 88–9, 99, 125–6, 133
instrumental versus expressive behavior, 12, 56, 79, 99
intercollegiate sport, 45, 65, 80; see also National Collegiate Athletic Association
interlocking systems of oppression, 3, 12, 19, 109, 126, 135
International Association of Athletics Federations (IAAF), 68, 69, 111, 112, 113, 114
International Olympic Committee (IOC), 3, 4, 7, 9, 20–6, 30, 41, 42, 44, 46, 53–9, 64, 68, 69, 75, 76, 78, 109, 111, 112, 113, 114, 117–18, 123–4, 133
international sport federations (IFs), 4, 8, 23, 30, 54, 112, 135
intersectional analysis, 4, 6, 7, 12, 18, 34
intersexed, 16, 113–14
Inuit, 54, 61; see also Indigenous peoples/Native peoples
Italy, Italian, 68, 75, 76

Japan, Japanese, 60, 70
Jewish people, 54–7, 77, 119
Johnson, Ben, 22
journalists, 3, 8, 33, 45, 57, 58, 63, 65, 74, 79, 92, 97, 99, 101, 103, 118, 133

Károli, Béla and Márta, 93, 116
Kellerman, Annette, 29, 89, 95
Kenya, Kenyan, 31–2
Korbut, Olga, 64, 116

law, legislation, 38, 42, 80, 119, 120, 122, 123, 124
lesbian/gay/bisexual/transgendered (LGBT) people, 13, 29, 31, 54, 97
lesbians, lesbianism, 6, 7, 13, 18, 26, 29, 30, 40, 53, 54, 57, 58, 72, 74, 104, 110, 111, 118, 119, 120–1, 133
lobbying, 41, 42, 46, 68, 114, 123
London 2012 Summer Olympic Games, 13, 123, 134
Lopiano, Donna, 45–6
Los Angeles 1932 Summer Olympic Games, 69, 71, 76
Los Angeles 1984 Summer Olympic Games, 133
Lum, Kristina, 96–7, 100

Maccabiah Games, 54, 56, 67
marketing, 26, 46, 48, 77
masculinities, 12–17, 22–6, 29, 56, 77, 101, 102, 109, 135
mass media, 3, 5, 9, 15, 16, 22, 23, 92, 103, 133
medical issues, 26, 27, 28, 69, 74, 109, 113, 114
mega-events, 2, 109, 122, 123
menarche, menstruation, 110, 116
metrosexuals, 27, 96, 103, 104
Mexico City 1968 Summer Olympic Games, 78
middle-class people, 2, 7, 40, 56, 58, 73, 79, 126
military, militarism, 23, 55, 76
Mitcham, Matthew, 97
Montreal 1976 Summer Olympic Games, 98, 120, 121
Moscow 1980 Summer Olympic Games, 53, 80
multiculturalism, 19

DOI: 10.1057/9781137291141

muscles, muscularity, 15, 16, 18, 28, 55, 56, 62, 63, 64, 70, 77, 94, 95, 109, 110, 112, 115, 116, 132
Muslims, Islamic, 23, 44, 47–8, 61, 89
myths, mythology, 25, 62, 63, 67, 75, 79, 95, 115

National Broadcasting Company (NBC), 46, 97
National Collegiate Athletic Association (NCAA), 45, 91
National Hockey League (NHL), 25, 101
national icons, 15, 26, 75, 76, 77, 133
national identity, 22, 75
nationalism, 8, 22, 55, 77, 124
Navratilova, Martina, 15, 16, 64
Nazi Olympics, see Berlin 1936 Summer Olympic Games
Nazis, 31, 57, 67, 76, 119
New York, 40, 67, 78, 121
newspapers, 33, 47, 63, 68, 73, 96, 98, 113
Nike, 17, 63
nudity, 28, 29, 89, 104, 111, 132
Nurmi, Paavo, 75, 90

obesity, 91, 110, 116
Olympic bids, 2, 3, 9, 57, 60, 61, 117, 118, 133
Olympic brand/branding, 19, 54, 68
Olympic "legacy," 21, 99
Olympic Project for Human Rights (OPHR), 78
Olympic Resistance Network (ORN), 126
Olympic values, 19, 53
opening ceremony, 13, 61
OutSports, 29–30
Owens, Jesse, 71, 77–8

Paralympic Games, 6
Paris 1924 Summer Olympic Games, 67, 68, 77
people with disabilities, 6, 18, 53
performance-enhancing drugs, 9, 31, 44, 91, 93, 94, 109, 112, 115, 116, 125

physical education, 23, 48
physical recreation, 8, 25, 41, 55, 65
physiology, 31, 95, 114
Pickett, Tydie, 71
police, 119–25
politicians, 59, 118, 120, 122, 123
pornography, 27–9
poverty, 33, 60, 119, 122, 123, 126
professional sport/athletes, 23, 27, 32, 45, 55, 59, 71, 89, 91, 95, 118
profit, 46, 119, 135
propaganda, 119, 133
protest, protesters, 21, 53, 57, 67, 78, 79, 112, 114, 119, 121, 135
puberty, 116–17

Qatar 2022 World Cup, 118

racialized bodies, 22, 26, 126
racism, 5, 7, 8, 19, 23, 31, 32, 40, 45, 57, 60, 61, 65, 71, 78, 79, 80, 94, 95, 99, 100, 112, 113, 119, 125, 126, 132
radical feminism, radical feminists, 2, 3, 5, 9, 40, 45, 46, 58, 126, 134
records, sporting, 20, 24, 55, 59, 66, 68, 70, 71, 72, 89, 112
recreation, 3, 21, 41, 67, 88, 110
reform, and the International Olympic Committee, 3, 40, 44, 45, 68
religion, 47, 48, 56, 77, 122
reproductive function, 15, 74, 109, 110
resistance, 3, 4, 5, 6, 9, 14, 20, 26, 43, 49, 126, 132–4
rhythmic gymnastics, 24, 46
role models, 21, 33, 40, 55
Romani peoples, 61, 122
Rosenfeld, Fanny, 72–4
rowing, rowers, 46, 80
Royal Canadian Mounted Police (RCMP), 120–1
Russia, Russian, 55, 59, 60, 76, 94, 116

Sagi, Ana Maria, 57, 58
Saudi Arabia, 47
scientific racism, 31, 60
Scott, Rose, 65, 89, 92

DOI: 10.1057/9781137291141

self-esteem, 16–18, 63, 72
Semenya, Caster, 16, 72, 109, 111–16
Seoul 1988 Summer Olympic Games,
    22, 121
sex trade workers, prostitutes, 9, 27, 63,
    98, 109, 118–25, 134
sex trafficking, 9, 122–3, 134
sexism, 19, 23, 45, 101, 124
sexual abuse, 91, 123; see also abuse
sexual harassment, 41, 91, 93, 109,
    118, 123
sexual minorities, 6, 54, 109, 119, 135
sexual orientation, 9, 13, 17, 97, 110, 111
sexual revolution, 29, 110
shooting, 23, 65
ski jump, 9, 42, 109, 123–6
Smith, Kenyon, 96
soccer, 46, 47, 55, 57, 104
social change, 26, 40, 77
social control, 63, 94
social justice, 7, 53
social media, 4, 9, 13, 133–5
social psychology, 4, 7, 12, 16, 18
social structures, 7, 16, 19, 23, 34, 132
socialism, 2, 9, 20, 55, 126
socioeconomic status, social class, 2, 3,
    18, 19, 40, 125, 126
softball, 46, 47, 70, 71, 110
solidarity, 9, 55, 69, 78, 79, 101, 121, 124
South Africa, South African, 16, 53, 55,
    72, 78, 112, 116
Spain, Spanish, 57–8, 121
sponsors, 3, 6, 21, 24, 27, 44–5, 47, 48,
    61, 63, 98, 99, 102, 109
sport bikinis, 46–7
sport celebrities, 21, 27, 28, 32, 34, 77,
    80, 100, 103
sport feminists, 3, 9, 41, 42, 43, 49, 58,
    109, 123, 135
sport history, history, 3, 5, 43, 58, 61, 62,
    67, 73, 74
sportification, sportization, 8, 20, 24
sportive movement, 12, 19, 20, 25, 132
sports clubs, 70, 80, 95, 96, 99
sports fans, spectators, 23, 47, 48, 55,
    58, 62, 65, 68, 88, 99, 119

St. Louis 1904 Summer Olympic
    Games, 60, 63, 66
stereotypes, 8, 23, 56, 60, 101, 104
steroids, 22, 94, 112, 115; see also
    performance-enhancing
    drugs
Stockholm 1912 Summer Olympic
    Games, 65–6, 90
Stojko, Elvis, 101
Stokes, Louise, 71
street sweeps, 109, 119
surveillance, 13, 15, 18, 22, 24, 33, 112
Sweden, Swedish, 65, 118
swimming, 5, 8, 13, 23, 29, 31, 47,
    64–8, 77, 80, 88–98, 99, 101, 103,
    104, 117
swimsuits, 29, 64, 66, 89–90, 98
Sydney 2000 Summer Olympic
    Games, 21, 22, 30, 60, 66, 89,
    114, 133, 134
symbolic representations, 7, 12, 19,
    22–3, 34, 132
symbols, 17, 22, 60–1, 62, 67, 76, 134
synchronized swimming, 8, 24, 46, 76,
    95–8, 100, 103, 104

Tarzan films, 77, 80
television coverage, 15, 23, 24, 44, 45,
    93, 102, 103, 132, 135
tennis, 15, 23, 45, 64, 70, 72, 73, 80,
    90, 99
testosterone, 113, 115
thinness, 17, 18, 91
Thorpe, Jim, 59
Title IX, 42, 80
Tokyo 1964 Summer Olympic Games,
    13, 75, 118
"tomboy" label, 15, 72, 110
tourism, 3, 120, 122
track and field events, 5, 23, 28, 63, 64,
    68, 69, 70, 71, 73, 74, 76, 80,
    116, 125
transnational feminism, 2, 3, 5, 42
transsexuals, 114, 127n18
Turino 2006 Winter Olympic Games,
    102

DOI: 10.1057/9781137291141

United States (US), 2, 21, 28, 32, 42, 45,
    46, 53, 56, 57, 61, 67, 68, 69, 70,
    71, 77, 78, 80, 88, 93, 94–5, 97,
    98, 101, 102, 110, 119
United States Olympic Committee
    (USOC), 67, 119
universities, 42, 104, 111, 115
USSR, 94

Valla, Trebisonda, 76
Vancouver 2010 Winter Olympic
    Games, 9, 30, 42, 61, 101, 102,
    109, 123–6, 133, 135
violence, 42, 55, 101, 109, 123, 125, 126
virilizing effects, of doping, 94, 112
voting rights, 67, 68

Weir, Johnny, 102–3
Weissmuller, Johnny, 29, 75, 77,
    80
Williams, Esther, 76, 95
Winter Olympic Games, 30,
    99–104, 109, 125; see also
    Vancouver 2010 Winter
    Olympic Games
working-class people, 7, 23, 42, 54, 55,
    56, 63, 67, 70, 72, 73, 94, 95, 99,
    101, 119, 123, 135
World War I, 4, 53, 56
World War II, 4, 53, 56

YWCA, YMCA, 70, 94
YWHA, 70, 94

DOI: 10.1057/9781137291141

CPSIA information can be obtained at www.ICGtesting.com
Printed in the USA
LVOW08*1455271213

367126LV00006B/102/P